D1738746

Up and to the Right
The Story of John W. Dobson
and His Formula Growth Fund

UP
and to the
RIGHT

THE STORY OF JOHN W. DOBSON
AND HIS FORMULA GROWTH FUND

CRAIG TOOMEY

Published for the John Dobson Foundation by
McGill-Queen's University Press
Montreal & Kingston • London • Ithaca

ISBN 978-0-7735-4379-9 (cloth)
ISBN 978-0-7735-9186-8 (ePDF)
ISBN 978-0-7735-9187-5 (ePUB)

Legal deposit first quarter 2014
Bibliotèque nationale du Québec

Printed in Canada on acid-free paper that is 100% ancient forest free (100% post-consumer recycled), processed chlorine free.

McGill-Queen's University Press acknowledges the support of the Canada Council for the Arts for our publishing program. We also acknowledge the financial support of the Government of Canada through the Canada Book Fund for our publishing activities.

Library and Archives Canada Cataloguing in Publication

Toomey, Craig, author
    Up and to the right : the story of John W. Dobson and
        his Formula Growth Fund / Craig Toomey.

    Includes index.
    ISBN 978-0-7735-4379-9 (bound)

    1. Dobson, John W. 2. Formula Growth Limited – Biography.
    3. Capitalists and financiers – Canada – Biography. 4. Philanthropists – Canada –
    Biography. I. Title.

HG172.D63T66 2013   332.092   C2013-907303-5

Produced for McGill-Queen's University Press by
Focus Strategic Communications Incorporated.
Interior Design and Layout by Rob Scanlan

This book was typeset in 11/15 Sabon.

NB: All $ values refer to US dollars unless stated otherwise.

Acknowledgments

The author would like to give thanks and praises to the following people for providing helpful input, comments, and support in the research and writing of this book: René Catafago, Barbara Ellis, Michael Gentile, Kim Holden, Ari Kiriazidis, Randy Kelly, John Liddy, Rodney McCollam, Bette Lou Reade, and Rosanna Vitale from Formula Growth; Ian Soutar and Ian Aitken from Pembroke Management; Reuven Brenner from McGill University; and Diana and Parker Knox. Thank you to Los Angeles-based William O'Neil + Company for supplying company stock charts. Very special thanks to Alan Freeman for helping to reorganize and simplify the manuscript and for his skilful editing. Thanks as well, of course, to John Dobson, without whom none of this would have been possible, and to Mark Abley and Adrian Galwin at McGill-Queen's University Press for shepherding the manuscript into print. Last, but not least, thanks to my beloved wife, Rekha, for encouraging me to never give up.

Contents

Foreword

John Dobson was many things: a brilliant investor, an outstanding leader, a generous philanthropist. But, above all, he was a trusted and loyal friend whom I knew and admired for many years.

I am pleased that John's story is finally being told, although saddened that, having passed away on 30 July 2013, he did not live to hold this book in his hands. During his remarkable life, his contributions to entrepreneurship, to business education, and to the mentoring and advancement of young people were considerable. Yet these accomplishments rarely received the recognition they deserved.

John's success as an investor was extraordinary. At the same time, he tirelessly promoted entrepreneurship, which he believed was the best way to create wealth for Canadians, and he supported many groundbreaking entrepreneurial studies programs at McGill and other universities across Canada. In addition, he provided financial assistance that made it possible for scores of young people to attend university. Yet John always kept a low profile – rarely speaking in public or giving interviews – preferring to focus more on satisfying his clients than his ego, and devoting his energy to helping others.

His reluctance to be in the spotlight is reflected in the fact that he took little interest in telling the story of his life and his Formula Growth Fund. (He would have preferred to write what he called a "booklet" on the basics of investing and money management for the benefit of children as young as four.) As a result, this story has had to rely heavily on John's many friends and colleagues to recount, in their own words, what he meant to them and how he made an important difference in their lives.

A much deserved tribute, this book tells the fascinating tale of a great Canadian. For me, the underlying lesson is to always value your friends, never shy away from opportunity, and strive constantly to work for the greater good. This is John's message to us all, one well worth sharing.

His Excellency the Right Honourable David Johnston
Governor General of Canada

Preface

Memo to staff from John Dobson:

Objectives of Formula Growth Limited:

1. To make 20 per cent per year for our unit holders
2. To have fun doing it
3. To make certain that we have the people, discipline, and procedures to accomplish Objectives 1 and 2

Greed and fear. Many people cite these as the two main driving forces behind the stock market. But a successful investor should know that qualities such as vision, knowledge, discipline, risk tolerance, and patience are much more important.

John Dobson mastered all of these qualities to become one of Canada's greatest growth-stock investors. Over the past fifty years, a unit in his Formula Growth Fund has grown in value from the equivalent of $9 (CAN) to more than $5,400. An initial investment of $10,000 in Formula Growth in 1960 is worth today more than $6 million (CAN). In other words, it has increased an incredible 600 times! What's more, Formula Growth has lost none of John Dobson's magic. As this book went to print, according to *The Globe and Mail*'s Globe Investor, the fund ranked number one among Canadian investment firms managing US small- to mid-cap stocks, with a trailing one-year performance of 46 per cent through 30 September 2013. To increase 600 times is one thing, but to still be top of class after fifty-three years is priceless. It is the kind of performance that has earned the long-term loyalty of Formula Growth Fund unit holders, among them some of Canada's most prominent business people and entrepreneurs. It has also drawn the attention of several of the world's savviest investors, including the late Sir John

Templeton, who, at one time, was one of the largest Formula Growth unit holders.

The ride has not always been smooth. Nor has it been steady. Because Formula Growth invests almost exclusively in small to mid-cap high-growth stocks in the United States, the company has been prone to considerable volatility. It has been buffeted by economic, political, and social events as well as the occasional investment simply gone wrong. In the mid-1970s, during an especially severe stock market downturn that had a serious impact on Formula Growth, there was even a failed attempt to oust John Dobson from the Fund's management.

But he persevered through it all, never losing faith in the stock market, in his investment formula, in the magic of compound investing, in the advantages of risk tolerance, and in his hand-picked team of portfolio managers, administrators, and support staff. A man of considerable energy, skill, and generosity, John Dobson developed an extraordinary network of investment brokers, advisors, and experts stretching across North America and abroad, and cultivated relationships that endured for over half a century. His remarkable acumen for building an investment firm with exceptional professionalism, excellence, and savvy embedded in its DNA also paved the way for Formula Growth to launch a hedge fund in the early 2000s that has also become the envy of an industry too often riddled with failure.

One of John's favourite expressions was KISS – Keep It Simple, Stupid. He picked a career that was anything but simple, deciding to compete with the best and brightest on Wall Street. And while the academics, professors, analysts, and consultants concluded that the market was too smart and too efficient to beat, he proved them all wrong. He not only beat the market, he pulverized it. He did this through KISS – he always stayed calm, and he never wavered. KISS is devilishly hard to do, especially when it comes to investing real money – yours or other people's. But John was a master at it.

John's two overarching principles of investment were really simple: one, invest with good people running businesses that are growing fast; and two, always look forward and never look back. He never cared about the tiny details, the current quarter, or the latest macro concern being touted by the talking heads on TV. He nagged everyone at Formula Growth to always look to the next year, and even the two years after that, when calculating target prices for stocks in the portfolio.

John's "potential sheets" (spreadsheets that expressed a target price for every stock in the portfolio) were held in great reverence at Formula Growth. They were something akin to the Holy Grail. He obsessed over these sheets and targets. He grilled the team if the targets made no sense. Through these sheets, he forced us to peer into the future, no matter how cloudy, and take a shot at where the company or the stock would be by then.

We were not allowed to be cautious. We had to take some risk; otherwise, there could be no reward. John always reminded us that there were no rich pessimists. He wanted us to hit the ball straight down the fairway, and he wanted us to hit it a long way. He would browbeat us if we sold too soon because he knew the math of compounding could not work its magic on our returns if we were out of stocks prematurely.

But John would never admonish us if we made honest mistakes. As with the game of golf, he expected some bad shots; he understood that the investment business is just too tough not to have them. If we hit the ball into the woods or the sand, he simply expected us to get it back in play and make the most of it. And he expected us to finish the round, to see it through. Unlike the occasional mulligan at his favourite golf club, Mount Bruno, there are no mulligans in the stock market. And there was no such thing as quitting for John Dobson. In the end, he believed investing was a "numbers" game. You will never bat a thousand, but, as in golf, if you have some fundamentals like a good grip, posture, and swing plane, along with a good work ethic and nerve, you will post some solid scores. In his investing career, John posted many, many good scores, as he did on the golf course.

The principle of supporting good people and looking forward, never back, also permeated John's lifelong philanthropic work. He knew that if he encouraged passionate and energetic people, especially young people, we could build a better world by creating more leaders. This encouragement was obvious in the spectacular work he did through his John Dobson Foundation and through his personal generosity.

Thanks to the Foundation, John had a remarkable influence on generations of new entrepreneurs throughout North America and backed numerous organizations extolling the virtues of free-market capitalism. In 1989, the Foundation established the innovative Dobson Centre for Entrepreneurial Studies at McGill University, spawning similar centres at nearly two dozen universities across Canada. In addition, the Foundation supports entrepreneurial development at dozens of Canadian universities and colleges, as well as outreach programs, think-tanks, and other initiatives. These include or have included such varied groups as the Canadian Institute for Advanced Research, Youth Employment Services Montreal, and Junior Achievement of Canada. He was also the original sponsor of the Association of Collegiate Entrepreneurs (now Enactus Canada), a national student body that advocates entrepreneurial education. In recognition of his many contributions and achievements, John was awarded honorary doctorates from McGill, Concordia, Acadia, and Dalhousie universities. In 1997, he was named a Member of the Order of Canada and described as "a generous philanthropist [who] created a foundation to help develop entrepreneurial skills and self-sufficiency among Canadian youth."

Through it all, John constantly stressed to anyone who would listen the importance of common sense and having fun in life. His approach was "grip-it-and-rip-it," and have fun while you are doing it. When it came to fun, he had an almost obsessive passion for the game of golf that began in his youth. He played on over 600 of the leading courses throughout the world, was a long-time board member of the Royal Canadian Golf Association, and helped run the

Canadian Open. He even served for a time as a highly respected *Golf Digest* course rater for Canadian and US golf courses, and he was not shy about complaining of the unnecessary difficulty of some greens. Golf played an important role in helping John develop business relationships and loyal friendships that endured for over half a century. He described it as a networking game played all over the world.

In addition to golf and work, John devoted a tremendous amount of personal time to mentoring and teaching people. I experienced this guiding hand of "Mr D" first-hand. He focused on me and taught me everything he knew. He pushed and challenged me. As a great networker, he introduced me to everyone – and he seemed to know everyone. He was Facebook and LinkedIn and the World Wide Web all rolled into one. He worked a room better than anyone I ever knew. Amazingly, he did it the old-fashioned way, as he never had a cellphone or even a computer. I was lucky. When I met my boss over thirty years ago, I won the lottery. What skills I have today, I owe them all to Mr D.

We had all hoped that John would live long enough to be able to hold this book in his hands, but sadly, he passed away on 30 July 2013, just five days after his eighty-fifth birthday. I will miss him deeply, as will his entire second family at Formula Growth. But we can take some solace in the fact that we can finally reveal the never-before-told story of John Dobson and his Formula Growth Fund – a fund that throughout the past fifty years, despite uncertainty, upheaval, and shocks on the world stage, has consistently headed in one direction: *Up and to the Right.*

Randall W. Kelly
President
Formula Growth Limited

15 October 2013

Even when he was a little boy, John Dobson's forthright personality was obvious to see.

Young John with a grapefruit — a rare treat in 1934 — and his family's big car.

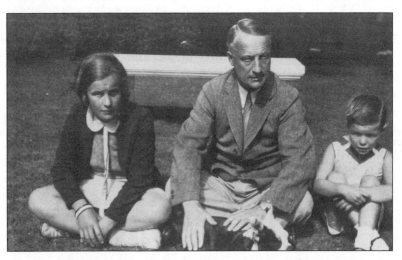

John is on the right of this picture, together with his sister, Virginia, and his father, Sydney Dobson.

Since you cannot play golf in a Montreal winter, young John turned his attention to hockey.

Fortunately, the snow would eventually melt and allow John to pick up his golf clubs.

John with his friend Jacques Tétrault and two young women, one of them feeding a piglet in the landmark Montreal restaurant Au Lutin Qui Bouffe.

John Dobson, the quintessential
young businessman.

John, his sister, and his mother. The young man's
fixed smile seems aimed at his mother's hat.

On the practice tee at the Mount Bruno
Country Club.

At the Royal Montreal Golf Club in 1980, helping
run the Canadian Open.

As the friendly inscription shows, Dobson was on excellent terms with Canadian prime minister Brian Mulroney.

Confronting Sir Richard Branson, founder of the Virgin Group.

Receiving the Order of Canada from Governor-General Roméo Leblanc.

In 1996, McGill University awarded Dobson an honorary doctorate of law. Here he is with McGill's chancellor, Gretta Chambers.

The Formula Growth family, circa 2000: Seated from left to right are John Dobson; Kimberley Holden, vice-president (now retired); Randall W. Kelly, chief executive officer and co-chief investment officer; René Catafago, executive vice-president and chief financial officer; and standing are Anthony T. Staples, vice-president and senior portfolio manager; and John Liddy, co-chief investment officer and executive vice-president.

To the end of his life, golf remained one of John Dobson's passions.

UP
and to the
RIGHT

THE STORY OF JOHN W. DOBSON
AND HIS FORMULA GROWTH FUND

CHAPTER I

An Uncommon Man

John W. Dobson was a study in contrasts. A wealthy man who always shunned luxuries and conspicuous signs of wealth. An extremely generous man who saw frugality as the ultimate virtue. A highly sociable and, at times, gregarious individual who nevertheless always lived alone and did not enjoy being the centre of attention. A life-long bachelor who often relied heavily on the support of women and who took a keen interest in the careers and goals of young people. An affable person who could also be temperamental, impatient, and unwilling to suffer fools. An outstanding investor who made much of his money bringing new technologies to life but resisted most of them himself – he would always choose a smart conversation over a smart phone. An energetic and curious student whose 1949 McGill University yearbook quote paraphrased George Bernard Shaw: "Activity is the road to knowledge." He followed this maxim over the next six decades.

Talk to friends and colleagues about John Dobson, this man of contrasts, and they all agree that he was consistent about the three main passions in his life: work, the promotion of entrepreneur-ship, and the game of golf. He pursued all three with remarkable energy, dedication, and enthusiasm, adhering to the highest standards of honesty and integrity. In the process, he had a huge impact on those whose lives he touched, earning their unwavering loyalty and respect.

"John really was in many ways a very decent, honest, and fine example of mankind," says legendary Montreal money manager Stephen Jarislowsky, who knew Dobson since the early 1950s. "He was John, period. There were not too many people in his mould. I especially admired him as a decent human being, as someone who was trying to make a difference. He spent his whole life trying to change things in Canada for the better, whether it was entrepreneurship, or business, or politics. He had very strong values, which are hard to modify or shake."

While Dobson always demonstrated an unrelenting dedication to work in the service of his Formula Growth clients, he was also a strong believer in the importance of enjoying yourself, both on and off the job. "John always advised me to have a balanced approach," says Ian Soutar, his long-time colleague and friend. "He'd say: 'You can't spend all of your time in the office worrying about stocks. You've got to get out, travel a bit, and play some golf.' John kept his life very simple. It was golf and it was the investment business. I think that's one of the reasons why he was as successful as he was."

John Liddy, executive vice-president of Formula Growth, notes that simplicity was a hallmark of Dobson's life. Despite his considerable wealth, he stayed in the same modest apartment for thirty years. "He never lived large at all. His own self-aggrandizement was never a part of what he was about. I can't think of many others like that. He was a real old-school generous guy."

While he spent time socializing and playing golf, work was often foremost on Dobson's mind, but there was not always a clear distinction between the two pursuits. "You were always challenged by John," says Peter Mackechnie, a former Formula Growth executive. "For example, he'd suggest an afternoon of golfing. But when we'd get back to the office, we'd go over what we called target sheets to assess stocks. It was a very serious attitude there. There was no fooling around when we were working on stocks because John believed so much that the unit holders deserved the best we could give them. And he gave a lot."

∞ PUNCTUALITY ∞

Dobson's energy was legendary – few could keep up with him. "He was always the last one in the room, looking for something to do," says Randy Kelly, who succeeded him as Formula Growth's president. "After a long night of business meetings or socializing, he would still get into the office right on time the next morning and be ready to go." In fact, one of Dobson's most intractable quirks was his obsession with being on time. "The number one lesson from him is the importance of punctuality," says his niece, Diana Knox. "In his mind, if you weren't punctual, you were showing the other person that their time is not as important as yours is. You had to always make sure you were on time for John, or heaven help you otherwise!"

Bette Lou Reade, a long-time Formula Growth portfolio manager, recalls accompanying Dobson and Ian Soutar on a business trip to Dallas, Texas, where a number of appointments had already been lined up. "The plane was late, and because we were staying for a couple of days, we had each checked in several suitcases. When the plane landed, John would not let us get our bags off the carousel. He insisted that we had to get in the limousine and make it to the meetings. So, the whole day I could not concentrate on a single company because I thought I was going to lose my suitcase. It was just sitting in Dallas Airport on the ruddy carousel! We went back to the airport that night, and, sure enough, there were the bags."

This unflinching dedication to punctuality even extended to leisure activities. "Sometimes we'd have a golf game. You'd get off a plane, and all John would do was go straight to where we were going to play golf," says Reade. "You could never eat, never had a chance to change. You just had to get there."

At times, some felt that Dobson's intolerance for tardiness bordered on rude, yet it was so extreme that it could sometimes be amusing. "I remember going one day to the Four Seasons Hotel in Montreal to pick up a friend of John's from California who was here to attend a meeting," says Barbara Ellis, Formula Growth's long-time office manager. "John had told his friend to meet us at 5:03 p.m., but at 5:05 p.m., he wasn't there, so John drove off. I said, 'He's only two minutes late! Can't we wait a bit?' 'Nope,' John replied. 'I told him 5:03. I gave him two minutes. He's late!' I don't know what happened to him, but I don't think he made the meeting."

Even though Formula Growth made many successful investments in technology firms, Dobson displayed a complete lack of interest in computers, mobile phones, or other modern communication devices. "John didn't keep up with information technology systems and never had a cellphone," notes Ian Soutar. "He was always quite resentful of the fact that when he'd come in to the office, people had no time to sit and talk to him. They'd be looking at their screens, emailing people, the kind of stuff that goes on in the real world. The whole information flow has changed now. It's so much quicker and so much more intense. Whether it's better or not, I don't know, but it's the way people operate today. His view was that we're really wasting our time too much, and there's a whole load of information that we can't process anyway."

Dobson, who never married, had a somewhat conflicted relationship with women. While relying on their support, especially from Formula Growth colleagues such as Barbara Ellis, Bette Lou Reade, and Kim Holden (Bette Lou's daughter and a one-time portfolio manager), when push came to shove, he preferred to deal with men, even at social occasions. "All John's stuff did not involve wives, so if we went to a hockey game or something, it would generally not be with wives because he didn't have one," says Peter Mackechnie. "He was all into business, growth, opportunities, and free enterprise, that kind of thing. He really didn't have time for women, but he enjoyed their company nevertheless."

Ian Soutar recalls that his former partner, the late Neil Ivory, once invited Dobson to have dinner with him and his wife. Dobson had a girlfriend with him, and he was going to a hockey game that evening. "They got through the main course, and the dessert was about to come. But John looked at his watch and said it was time to go to the hockey game. His date said it was impolite to leave, and she was going to stay for dessert. John said that was fine. He got up, left his date there and went to the hockey game by himself." Soutar says that this story reveals a lot about Dobson's character. "I think that if you are going to get married, if it's going to last, you're going to have to compromise. And he was not fond of compromising."

Dobson's unusual temperament was a source of bemusement among those who knew him well. "You could never foresee how John would react," says René Catafago, Formula Growth's long-time CFO and executive vice-president, who was also Dobson's personal financial and tax advisor. "He was very unpredictable. One time he gave me hell for ordering a new desk, saying it was a waste of money. Yet he could be so generous. He was also absent-minded. I remember one day he was in the boardroom and my office was not too far. I heard him scream for me, so I immediately jumped up and said, 'Yes, John?' He responded, 'Not now, I'm busy!'"

Sometimes Dobson's meticulousness and attention to detail, so critical to his success as an investor, could be maddening, according to René Catafago. "I once was at a meeting, giving John spreadsheets of companies I had analyzed. Everything was so neatly done with columns, ratios, and cash flow. It was a nice sheet per company. Everything was pluses and minuses, which were in brackets. I saw John looking very perplexed about the whole thing. He turned around and showed the sheet of paper to Ian Soutar and said, 'Ian, don't you think the way he does his brackets is funny?' I got so mad, I said, 'John, after all the work I have done, all you have to pick on is my brackets?'"

∽ GENEROSITY ∾

Despite his quirks, Dobson is fondly recalled for his generosity and concern toward others. "He genuinely cared about people in this organization and keeping everyone together," says Kim Holden. "He fostered this culture of togetherness, always asking how the day was going, how the evening and vacations were, and so on. He was very good about it." Dobson's generosity, often spontaneous, is legendary. "I had no money at all when I started, and the banks wouldn't give me a mortgage," says Bette Lou Reade, who was anxious to buy herself a home. "As soon as John heard about it, I got my mortgage."

"In the 1970s, John started providing financial assistance for youngsters, including the children of his friends who were attending university," says boyhood friend Robert Paterson. "No one knows how many he helped. He seemed uncomfortable with people being aware of his generosity, as this was a private matter with him."

Jim Durrell, a businessman and former mayor of Ottawa, knew Dobson since the 1950s when his father worked with Dobson at Dominion Engineering Works in Montreal. Durrell likes to tell a remarkable story about Dobson's impromptu approach to giving. It happened a few years ago after a game of golf at the Cape Breton resort of Baddeck, where John was having dinner with Kelvin Ogilvie, president of Acadia University (and now a member of the Canadian Senate), and Harvey Gilmour, an Acadia fundraiser at the time. "The maître d' came over after we had eaten and said he hoped we enjoyed the meal," Durrell recalls. "Kelvin mentioned that the waiter had done an outstanding job. The young fellow came over later to thank us for the compliment, and we asked him where he was going to school. He said he had wanted to go to Acadia, where his father had gone, but his family didn't have the money. He was working to save up for next year. Ogilvie gave him his card and said, 'I'm the president of Acadia. Your marks are all right?' He said yes, his marks were great. Then the Dobber [as Dobson is known to some intimates] chirped in: 'If your marks are good, then you have a four-year ride at Acadia courtesy of me.' The fellow graduated a couple of years ago and did exceedingly well."

There's a moral to this story, Durrell suggests. "I've since said to my kids: 'Treat everybody you deal with respectfully, because you never know who they may be.' My dad would always say, 'The world should be a better place because you've been here.' That's been a guiding principle for us throughout life. And there's no question the world has been a better place because the Dobber's been here."

Jim Durrell says that Dobson never hesitated to give you his straight and unedited opinions. "He didn't tell you what you wanted to hear, rather what he thought," Durrell says. He remembers toying with the idea of getting an MBA as a young man, and Dobson advised him not to, saying the degree was overrated. "He felt I should get out and work more. He said there were too many people with theories and not enough practical experience." Durrell formed his own business and later spent a lot of time with Dobson working on a business plan for a new concept. "Our idea was to privatize recreational facilities across Canada. John gave me advice and lent me some money as an investment. He has a powerful personality, but for all of his bluster, he was as compassionate and caring an individual as you can find. If someone asked what I admired about John, I'd say his philanthropy, and his assistance to people was consistent and always without fanfare." Durrell eventually sold the recreational company to a US buyer. He went on to become a prominent member of Ottawa's business community, serving as president of the Ottawa Senators hockey team and chairman of the Ottawa International Airport Authority, as well as spending five years as the city's mayor.

While Dobson usually limited his giving to entrepreneurial or academic pursuits, he was sometimes willing to bend the rules. Nancy Durrell McKenna, Jim's sister, approached Dobson in 1996 about an idea for improving the health of mothers in Africa. She had a chance to work on a project in Ghana and asked Dobson if he would be willing to give her $50,000. "He said I wasn't an entrepreneur and he wasn't supporting maternal health, but he told me he supported me as an individual. A charity in Canada was able to accept his donation, and it was given to me then to do the work," she recalls. Today, Nancy Durrell McKenna is executive director of SafeHands for Mothers, a UK-based charity that supports safe maternal health practices in developing countries. "The most important lesson I learned from John was giving. He had a huge philanthropic spirit. He supported entrepreneurs and put many people through university. Giving back was very, very important to him."

Prominent research scientist Sam Catherine Johnston was another recipient of Dobson's generosity. Despite her somewhat less-than-stellar academic performance at McGill, he backed her in the pursuit of a doctorate at Harvard. Her goal was to design, implement, and evaluate a global development program for mental-health policy planners and doctors who care for refugees and assist people in post-conflict areas. "Where most people who would provide a scholarship for a young person would look first and foremost for a perfect academic record, which I did not have upon graduating from McGill, Mr Dobson instead paid attention to my work in education in the two years after I graduated, as well as my strong desire to do something innovative. Global Mental Health Program trains fifty doctors around the world, a testament to Mr Dobson's generosity and his willingness to take risks in investing in young minds."

Florence Tracy, retired director of McGill Residences, credited John's generosity with the ability to provide numerous McGill students with needed bursaries. "John donated [money] to McGill for me to use without restrictions and to disburse according to my own discretion," she wrote on the occasion of Dobson's eightieth birthday. "One student applied for a Rhodes Scholarship in the Caribbean region but was unable to afford to travel home for the interview. Thanks to John, she was able to attend and become the first woman from the Caribbean to be selected as a Rhodes Scholar." Tracy noted that Dobson also funded the establishment of computer labs at six McGill residence halls in 1996, long before students routinely arrived with PCs. Alex K. Paterson, a prominent Montreal lawyer and former chair of McGill University's Board of Governors (and the cousin of Dobson's boyhood friend Robert Paterson), noted on the same occasion that hundreds of students across Canada received the benefit of Dobson's generosity. "A lot (was) done anonymously. Many others benefited from his investment advice for over half a century and were guided not only by John's investment wisdom, but by his counsel on a litany of subjects."

Dobson's support for young people was consistent throughout his long career. Philippe Hynes is a prime example. He first met Dobson while he was working as a bartender at Dobson's beloved Mount Bruno Country Club near Montreal. Later, while at Concordia University, Hynes participated in a Formula Growth-sponsored portfolio management competition, and Dobson became his mentor. "He gave me advice on where to go for a master's degree," Hynes recalls. "I had been accepted to Boston College, and he offered to pay. But after making some phone calls, he said that is doesn't matter if the university you go to is not one of the top twenty. Because of his advice, I decided to go to L'École des hautes études commerciales (HEC) in Montreal, which turned out to be the best decision." By staying in Montreal and getting to know investment firms there, Hynes positioned himself for a successful career. After working for Van Berkom and Associates Inc., he co-founded Tonus Capital Inc., an investment and portfolio fund manager. But Dobson was still there for him. "John invested in our fund, which is a great reference to have in Montreal. He was so well respected, and his involvement gave us credibility."

Hynes retains enormous respect for Dobson and remains forever grateful for his backing. "He was always there to guide me. He was very generous with his time and money." Hynes was not a member of the Mount Bruno Golf Club, but in 2008, Dobson even sponsored his wedding reception there. "He invited me to play golf that morning with my father and father-in-law. It was quite a thrill."

∽ PHILANTHROPY ∾

Diana Knox considers her Uncle John to be a "genuine philanthropist" who did things quietly and often anonymously. After graduating from high school, she decided to study languages in Switzerland for a year. She suspected her uncle helped finance the trip, but no one ever told her directly. On her return, she enrolled at a university in New Brunswick and there met her future husband, Parker Knox.

"We have instilled an interest in travel and languages in our own kids, and I think this interest goes back to John. All of this happened because of him," she says.

Parker Knox says Dobson has also been a marvellous role model for him, especially when it comes to leadership. "While leadership is fundamental in business, Dobson believed it is lacking in today's world," he says. "Many people will think of him as an entrepreneur, but his views on leadership were fundamental." Dobson's belief in being ethical in business still inspires Knox. "If I had trouble with how to handle a business situation, John would counsel me by asking me good questions, but never clearly telling me what to do. He led me through a process of discovery. He didn't tell me what to think, but told me about different perspectives to view the issue from."

This humility is a constant theme for those who knew Dobson. "John was very blunt and direct, but also highly trustworthy," says Reuven Brenner, the REPAP chair of economics at McGill's management faculty and a long-time Dobson confidante. "He was very humble and modest. You discovered his giving almost by accident. He was one of the few who practised what he preached."

Brenner remembers first meeting Dobson when he was moving into his McGill office more than twenty years ago. "The boxes had just arrived at my office. I was unpacking when John knocked at the door. He came in and said, 'I am John Dobson. Go on doing what you're doing.' I had no idea who he was. I asked the dean, who told me, 'Don't ask questions. Just keep him happy. He's one of our biggest donors.' I do not know if I managed that, but it was the beginning of a long, close friendship."

William I. Turner Jr, a board member of the John Dobson Foundation for many years, says he thinks that what Dobson did with his money was selfless, and he has helped to influence generations of new entrepreneurs throughout North America. "He was a very good judge of people. On occasions, he was a little impatient of stupidity. He deserved his good friends. He worked hard for them."

"He was a loyal man, so he had very many loyal friends," agrees John Turner, the former Canadian prime minister, who could rely on strong support from Dobson throughout his political career. "I was a friend of his for nearly seventy years. We shared a lot of confidences. We saw eye to eye on most issues."

Affable. Temperamental. Loyal. Unpredictable. Generous. Shrewd. John Dobson's diverse qualities made him one of the most intriguing business personalities ever to emerge in Canada. And none of it would have been possible without the lessons and values instilled in him at a young age by the most important person in his life: his father.

CHAPTER 2

A Father's Son

*An honest day's work for an honest day's pay is still a
good recipe for prosperity, perhaps the only formula
that will ensure lower prices, a higher standard of
living, and lasting good times for all.*

— SYDNEY GEORGE DOBSON

When John Dobson was a boy, his father would set aside $100 in
shares every year in his name. "They belonged to me, but father
wouldn't let me touch them or do anything with them," John
recalled. "We would sit around and discuss the investments and why
he made them. But that was it." Finally, when John turned eighteen,
his father gave him access to the funds, which had grown into a tidy
sum thanks to the magic of compounding. John promptly decided to
invest most of it in a silica mine headed by a friend. "When my father
heard about my plans, he said, 'No silica company has ever made
money in Quebec,'" John would later remember. "He would make
subtle comments like that but never direct me to do something. So I
bought the shares and lost all my money." That first investment over
sixty years ago taught him a valuable lesson about risk and reward,
the importance of properly doing your homework, and the value of
obtaining expert advice from others.

In many ways, the foundation for John Dobson's success lay with
his father, Sydney George Dobson, whose initial guidance on the
merits of saving and investing was one of many influences on his
son. An unassuming man who worked for more than fifty years at
the Royal Bank of Canada, Sydney Dobson rose from a lowly clerk
to become its president and chairman. He epitomized many of the

personality traits and beliefs that John held dear throughout his life: the importance of self-reliance, hard work and entrepreneurship, a suspicion of big government and abhorrence of over-taxation, a keen interest in young people, and a selfless generosity toward others. "I'm living life as my father's son all the time," John would say. "He had a great deal of common sense and knew everybody worth knowing in Canada, from Louis St Laurent to C.D. Howe. You can't get a better deal than that and would be a fool not to benefit from it."

Sydney Dobson was born on 20 September 1883. He was the youngest of five children of Job William Dobson, a wealthy marine contractor and farmer in Sydney, Nova Scotia, and his wife, Harriet Martell. At the age of seventeen, Sydney decided he was done with school and told his parents that he wanted to start working. His father tried to persuade him to go to college but, having failed in this, succeeded in getting young Sydney a job at the local branch of the Merchants' Bank of Halifax. That was in 1900, a year before it was renamed the Royal Bank of Canada. Organized in 1864 by seven merchants who needed a bank for their foreign business, Merchants was already the largest banking organization in Canada and twelfth largest in the world, with assets of over $2 billion.

The Dobson home was across the bay from the rapidly growing steel town, which meant that young Sydney had to row across the water to and from work, a story that remains legendary at the Royal Bank over a century later. He worked as much as twelve hours each day, most of the time delivering and collecting bank drafts. His salary was a princely $100 a year, or just under $2 a week.

After four years at the Sydney office, Dobson was transferred to Truro (further west in Nova Scotia) as ledger keeper, where he crossed paths for the first time with Morris W. Wilson, who was to become a trusted colleague and mentor. A future Royal Bank president, Wilson was an accountant at the branch and quickly marked Dobson for promotion, impressed by his "unusual qualities of application and accuracy," his penchant for hard work, and his conscientiousness.

Sydney Dobson was part of an extraordinary tradition of Maritime entrepreneurial genius, individuals whose business abilities, tremendous drive, and inexhaustible work ethic propelled them to the pinnacle of success in Canada and abroad. They included men such as Max Aitken, the New Brunswick schoolboy who became the British newspaper baron Lord Beaverbrook; his one-time partner, Izaak Walton Killam, who emerged from Yarmouth, Nova Scotia, to become Canada's leading industrialist; and Sir James Dunn, a New Brunswicker who made his fortune in mining, steelmaking, and shipping.

Over the next fifteen years, Sydney Dobson would rise rapidly through the ranks at the Royal Bank, criss-crossing Canada to assume management positions at branches across the country. In 1916, he was appointed manager of the Vancouver branch; then, two years later, he was transferred to the superintendent's department in Winnipeg. In 1919, Dobson was named general inspector at the Royal's headquarters, which had moved to Montreal from Halifax several years earlier. He was appointed assistant general manager in 1922 and general manager in 1934.

∞ THE MONTREAL MOVE ∞

William I. Turner Jr, former chairman of Consolidated-Bathurst Inc. and a friend of John Dobson for sixty years, recalls that Sydney Dobson's transfer to Montreal happened almost by chance and was the result of his impressive judgment of people, a trait shared by his son. "The story goes that head office had offered Sydney a job as manager of the main office in Hamilton, but had asked him to stop by in Montreal for a day for a chat. Sydney walked in, and the general manager told him that he had to replace the general inspector of the main branch in Montreal. Sydney was asked for his opinion of the selected candidates. He replied that he wouldn't choose any of them because none seemed to be qualified. Sydney returned to Hamilton, and when he arrived there, he found a telegram offering him the position in Montreal."

In Montreal, Sydney Dobson and his wife, Beatrice (née Chambers), settled into a comfortable apartment in Montreal's affluent "Square Mile" district on the slopes of Mount Royal, just west of McGill University. It was the home turf of Canada's business elite, where railway and industrial tycoons had built sprawling mansions in the nineteenth century. Some of these mansions were already starting to make way for elegant apartment blocks and office buildings after the First World War. The couple's daughter, Virginia, was born in 1921. John came along seven years later, on 25 July 1928.

Sydney Dobson continued to earn promotions, and by 1942, he was vice-president and general manager of the Royal Bank. Three years later, he was named executive vice-president, working as right-hand man to his old friend Morris Wilson, who had assumed the presidency in 1934. (Wilson was John's godfather.) The two colleagues appeared together on the last five-dollar banknote issued by the Royal Bank in 1943, marking the end of the era when Canada's chartered banks printed their own currency. The Bank of Canada, founded in 1934, gradually took over the responsibility for issuing currency.

In 1946, Wilson died suddenly, and the Royal Bank's board selected Sydney Dobson as his successor. "$100-a-Year Bank Clerk Now in President's Chair," proclaimed a 6 June article in the *Toronto Daily Star*. It was written by the financial editor, Beland Honderich, who would later rise to become chairman and publisher of Torstar, the parent company of the *Star*.

At sixty-three years old, Dobson was characterized as a modest man who was loath to speak about himself or his banking experience. Honderich described Dobson, the fifth president of the Royal Bank, as "a short, stocky man 5'7", 170 pounds, with steel-grey hair and hazel eyes" and "as friendly and informal as a prairie merchant." "He is recognized as a keen, forthright banker whose hard work has been the principal reason for his success." "He walks four miles each day to and from his St James Street office and his Sherbrooke Street apartment. It is a rare occasion when he rides, even during the cold winter. He smokes a pipe, but seldom at work, and flowers are taboo in his office except for May flowers once a year from the Maritimes," Honderich wrote.

Reporting on the new president's appointment, the *Montreal Gazette* described Dobson as "a virile man, active and endowed with an abundance of energy. He likes motoring long distances and has an itch for golf. His first love is the sea and the ships that ply upon it, and his greatest hobby, banking."

Away from the office, Sydney spent most of his time with his family. John's lifelong passion for golf was already in evidence, as one newspaper reported: "Although [Sydney Dobson] plays golf in the '80s, he has to admit that his son, John, 18, usually beats him. A Sunday morning during the summer usually finds father and son walking along the Montreal harbour just to look at the ships." On weekdays, Sydney would occasionally take his young son on visits to fire stations and local branches of the Royal Bank, where he would be greeted with the deference accorded to the bank's top executives. Sydney would also begin to explain to John how the bank worked. "During the war, father would tell me that the Canadian government would store its war plans in the bank's vaults for safekeeping overnight," John recalled. "That's how respected he was by the powers that be."

Sailing and sailboats were the pride and joy of Sydney Dobson's life. The walls of his office were lined with pictures of sailing vessels, including his own schooner, the Eskasoni, docked in his hometown of Sydney. (In 1954, the Dobson Yacht Club was established on land known as Shingle Point, which belonged to Sydney and his sisters. Today, Dobson Yacht Club describes itself as Cape Breton's premier yacht club.) "He lived on his boat for the two summer months each year that he could get away from the office and out to sea, often with daughter Virginia ... as his helper," one paper reported. One summer, when his only companion fell overboard in a heavy sea, Sydney skilfully manoeuvred the schooner and rescued him.

In 1946, another newspaper profile of Sydney, this time in the *St Maurice Valley Chronicle*, reported that the new Royal Bank of Canada president "is not the traditional banker type" and listed a number of traits that could later be said to characterize his son. "He is easy to meet, keenly aware of his responsibility as head of an institution serving the general public. His approach to problems is direct and incisive, his decisions quickly made," the *Chronicle* continued. John recalled that his father had a particular penchant for cars and sharing long drives with his chauffeur. "It was not unusual for him to get in the car with his driver and spend two days driving to Nova Scotia for a one-day meeting, and then spend two days coming back. That certainly wasn't my idea of fun, but he loved it!"

∞ COMMUNITY AND CHARITY WORK ∞

Setting an example for his children, Sydney Dobson was active in the community, chairing fundraising campaigns such as that of Montreal's Welfare Foundation and Federated Charities, a precursor to the United Way. Federated Charities funded the work of thirty-three humanitarian organizations, including those that served destitute families, helped homeless and neglected children, and provided health services, as well as promoting "character building" among the young.

Sydney Dobson also emerged as a Canadian pioneer in corporate sponsorship of sports. In a story that has become part of Olympic lore, Sidney Dawes, the head of the Canadian Olympic Committee, phoned Dobson in 1947 and pleaded desperately for the Royal Bank's help in getting the Canadian Olympic team to the 1948 Winter Games in St Moritz, Switzerland. The Olympic Games were just a short time away, and the team did not have enough money to make the long and costly journey. Dobson did not hesitate and saved the day with the needed financial support. This started a long tradition at the Royal Bank of supporting Canadian athletes in general and the Canadian Olympic team in particular.

Sydney was frequently outspoken on current events. He was strongly anti-Communist, fervently pro-business, and opposed to big government – all opinions his son, John, would echo. Appearing at his first Royal Bank annual meeting as president in January 1947, he provided his formula for future prosperity: increased industrial output, improved co-operation between management and labour, and substantial tax reductions. At the same time, he warned that lavish government expenditures, low productivity, and higher wages would never be the ticket to good times. He also railed against sloth. "I regret very much the irresponsible outlook many persons have regarding work and wages," he lamented. "I am one who also believes that the time will come again when possession of a job will be considered an asset, when having a little money as a standby will loom larger in people's minds than leisure hours." True satisfaction, Sydney maintained, can "only be found when the worker values mainly the work he does, and not how much he is able to compel the employer to pay. I believe in a high standard of living for everyone, and in leisure, but I am sorry to say that too many people today make high wages and plentiful leisure the greatest aims of their lives."

In a theme that would often be repeated in his speeches and writings, and later echoed throughout John's life as well, Sydney Dobson reaffirmed his strong faith in the free enterprise system. At these meetings, held in the aftermath of the Great Depression and the Second World War, he argued that "the experiences of the past few years have brought home to all of us the fact that business and industry exist to satisfy the needs of people. I believe that prosperous business conditions will be the bedrock upon which people will satisfy most of their other wants."

He denounced high taxes, a subject that would also become a passion of his son, who was especially opposed to capital gains taxes. In 1946, Sydney noted that taxes accounted for 24 per cent of national income, more than double the level in 1938, following big tax increases needed to pay for the war effort. "The withdrawal of this money constitutes a drag upon business," Sydney argued. "A

substantial reduction in taxes would give an incentive to individuals and to industry, encourage expansion and new ventures, encourage greater production and lower prices, and therefore prove an aid
toward a higher standard of living."

Sydney also frequently spoke out against restrictive trade practices and planned economies, which he said deprived the world of
freedom of development and expansion of business. Denouncing
"totalitarian" countries, he noted that the only two countries Europe
could turn to for help after the war were the democracies of the
United States and Canada. "It should be our objective to show that
free enterprise is the only economic system in the history of the world
flexible enough to change in keeping with the needs of its people."

Sydney Dobson consistently had an optimistic outlook about
Canada's economic prospects, a trait inherited by his son. "On the
whole, our Canadian people are sensible and sound," he told Royal
Bank shareholders at the 1947 annual meeting. "They are entertained
by pictures and stories of Utopia, but they know that success is not
made of dreams. The story of Canada's advancement is one of people
and resources and the ingenuity of the people in using the resources."

∽ THE DOBSON DIARY ∽

From 1938 to 1957, Sydney Dobson wrote a remarkable diary of over
300 pages, chronicling the events leading up to the Second World
War, the war years, and the following decade. In the diary, sometimes written with John at his side, he demonstrated an ability to see
through the fog to record events and interpret outcomes before they
happened.

Writing in the fall of 1938, Sydney saw that appeasement toward
the Nazis was a horrible mistake, noting that while Britain had been
preaching and acting for disarmament, Germany had continued to
rearm itself. Commenting on the Munich agreement negotiated by
British prime minister Neville Chamberlain in October of that year,
Sydney predicted that war was imminent. "Apparently, the cause of

the back down by Great Britain and France was that they were not ready. But will they be ready when the next crisis comes? Personally, I do not think that they will be, as it will come too soon. I fear that Chamberlain's 'Peace in our time' will not be realized."

The same perceptiveness was evident on the morning of 7 December 1941, when Sydney predicted that war between the United States and Japan would break out at any moment. Writing hours before news of the attack on Pearl Harbor, he stated, "The possibility of war between the United States and Japan is very near and may start at any time, perhaps in a day or two. I have been unable to believe all along that the Japs would be such damn fools, but there appears to be no limit to the arrogance of these people. I firmly believe the United States will have to fight them some day."

Sydney usually recorded the day's events in his diary in the evening after being chauffeured or walking home from the Royal Bank's head office on St James Street in the centre of Montreal's thriving financial district. The Square Mile, where the Dobson family lived for all of John's childhood, was only a few miles away. "We moved about every five years, including to a house on what was then known as Mountain Street and an apartment on Sherbrooke Street, but we always stayed in the same area," John later said. He remained loyal to the neighbourhood, living and working for decades in the same few blocks west of McGill University – blocks that are also within a short walking distance of Formula Growth's offices on Sherbrooke Street.

∞ A LIFE OF PRIVILEGE ∞

By all accounts, John's was a life of privilege, but also one instilled with sound values of honesty, hard work, and self-reliance that would serve as guideposts throughout his life. "John's father may have been paid $30,000 to $40,000 a year, so they were certainly affluent," says Robert Paterson, John's schoolboy friend who lived across the street from the Dobson family during the Second World War. "But the family was frugal and careful about saving money, as people from the Maritimes could be expected to be. They were far from flamboyant, which was considered in bad taste after the 1930s."

John was expected to earn his own pocket money and had a regular newspaper route. "One summer, I worked at the Dupuis Frères department store in downtown Montreal in an attempt to learn French, but I wasn't very successful," he chuckled. The family would often go away for a month at a time to Chester, Nova Scotia, where he would swim, play golf, practise his tennis, and mingle with family friends from Canada and the United States, many of them prominent citizens. In winter, they would go to the family cottage in the Laurentian village of Sainte-Adèle for cross-country skiing and other winter sports (a tradition that would endure for over seventy years).

Among John's earliest and closest friends were twin brothers André and Jacques Tétrault, who lived nearby in the Square Mile. "I was considered to be part of the Tétrault family," Dobson said. "I was always over at their house, being consulted on family affairs. We almost lived together. We played sports and sat around on street corners talking into the late evening. Those were good days."

"He was a very easygoing guy," says Jacques Tétrault, who would go on to found the well-known law firm of McCarthy Tétrault and to become a long-time director of Formula Growth. "We played cricket and soccer together, and later on, I helped him organize activities at McGill, such as the Winter Carnival. We grew up together and were always great pals." The trio all went to Selwyn House, a private boys' school. Dobson admitted to being an average student at the time, although in university, he would often score straight As. "I was middle range, but I was interested in everything that went on," he said. "I never finished first, but I had a lot of energy and enthusiasm. I was always running around doing something, but not necessarily being productive." John's mother would make sure he made it over to Selwyn House, which, at the time, was right across the backyard from their house (it later moved to Westmount). "Mother was a very good-looking, stay-at-home mom whom everyone adored," he recalled. "I was closer to father but always felt very fortunate to have such a wonderful mother."

Being a busy executive, Sydney had a laissez-faire approach to parenthood. "There was no time for him to discipline me," John admitted. Sydney was a supporter of the federal Liberal Party, a tradition later followed by John, though he generally steered away from active politics. "His political leanings would have been Liberal, since that was all that there was around at the time, and he was friends with many prominent Liberals such as Louis St Laurent and C.D. Howe," said John. "But he didn't do anything of substance in politics."

The Dobsons were good church-going Protestants, although John admitted that he opted out as soon as he could. After church on Sundays, the family would go to the Mount Bruno Golf Club for an afternoon game, allowing John to nourish a passion for golf that would remain with him throughout his life. "I started golf very early, at age eight or nine, and played my first game with a friend while my parents were off in Europe," John recalled. "I had a terrible start: it took me seventeen strokes to finish the first hole. I got better after that!"

Robert Paterson, who would cross paths with John throughout his life and have a long career at the Royal Bank, remembers that his friend was always keen on sports. "Everyone played hockey and baseball in his backyard," he says. Occasionally, the Selwyn House hockey team would cram into the Dobsons' large car with their duffel bags, skates, and sticks, to be driven by the family chauffeur to a local rink for practice.

Even though John and his sister, Virginia, were not that close in age – she was seven years older – they always had great admiration and respect for one another, and John would look out for her throughout her life. "Mother was very proud of John," according to Diana Knox, Virginia's only child. "They shared a passion for golf and family relationships." John's relationship with his parents followed the Victorian ideal "to be seen and not heard," and he always referred to them formally as "mother" and "father," Diana adds.

Virginia attended Miss Edgar's and Miss Cramp's School, a private girls' school, graduating in 1939, and she went on to attend McGill during the war. In 1943, she went to New York where she worked as a secretary for several years. Having returned to Montreal, in 1948, she married Stuart Cockfield, son of Harry Cockfield, the co-founder of prominent Montreal advertising agency Cockfield Brown. "Dad died very young, and my mother was left to raise me alone, with John stepping in as the father figure," says Diana Knox. She recalls her uncle fondly, but remembers him as someone who could be "very strict and stern about certain things. "I'd mostly see him up at the cottage in Sainte-Adèle on weekends, or at Mount Bruno." The contrast between John and Virginia was striking. "Although my mother was very approachable and emotional, John's life was always very regimented. As an adult, I think he just continued this and never displayed his emotional side."

After her father's early death, Diana Knox lived a comfortable life with her mother in Montreal's Town of Mount Royal, in a house that she says was probably bought for them by her grandfather, Sydney Dobson. He also provided financial support for Diana and her mother, although nothing was ever said about it. "As a single mum, I think Virginia did a great job of bringing me up. I never lacked anything. She instilled the values of hard work – there was no 'silver spoon in my mouth.' This all stemmed from my grandfather."

In 1955, when John was just twenty-seven, John's mother, Beatrice, died unexpectedly of complications from phlebitis. "It was a shock because she was five years younger than my father, and we thought he'd die before her," John said. In 1957, his father, Sydney, wrote an entry in his diary for the first time in two years: "My beloved wife for forty-two years suddenly passed away, and I have been far from normal for a long time," he said, explaining the long period of silence. Noting that he had also been in the hospital five times for kidney stones, he added that "I think it is understandable that, under all the circumstances, the diary should be forgotten."

John and Sydney continued to live together until the early 1960s. That was when Sydney fell ill with dementia and had to be placed in the Douglas Hospital, where he passed away on 8 August 1969.

"My grandfather had Alzheimer's for several years near the end, and my very patient mother would deal with him as he telephoned over and over asking the same questions," Diana Knox recalls. "When we'd visit his home before he entered the hospital, I would go ask my grandfather for five dollars. I'd wait ten minutes, then go back and ask for five dollars again because I knew by then he'd have forgotten."

A day after Sydney's death, the *Montreal Gazette* ran an obituary under the headline: "Outstanding Canadian banker dies age eighty-five." The subhead declared: "Career with RBC covered more than fifty years and extended from the lowest desk to the highest executive position." Earle McLaughlin, the Royal Bank's president and chairman, said: "No individual has contributed more to make the bank what it is today, and he holds a place in its history which will be everlasting."

∞ OFF TO MCGILL ∞

After their years at Selwyn House, the Tétrault brothers went to Lower Canada College, while John Dobson was sent to Trinity College School in Port Hope, Ontario, a not uncommon route for well-to-do Anglo-Montrealers who wanted their children to round out their Quebec high-school education, which ends at grade 11. "My mother had also been 'shipped off' to Toronto for grade 12," notes Diana Knox. "At the time, a lot of people who could do so sent their kids away to boarding school. In a sense, this helps before you go off to university." In those days, boarding schools were seen as good places for affluent parents to send their children, not only to gain a solid education, but also to learn the habits of independence."

In 1945, after a year at Trinity, John enrolled at McGill University to study commerce and immediately joined Delta Upsilon fraternity on the recommendation of Stuart Cockfield, his sister, Virginia's, future husband. "This was a very lucky break for me and somewhat of a turning point in my life," John said. "Upsilon was where all the student leaders were, where many of the big activities at McGill were organized. If I had joined any other fraternity, I would likely have spent a good deal of my time drinking with the other members! I wouldn't have become a leader and got into Harvard." Before long, John was organizing a variety of activities, including McGill Winter Carnival. "I was by far the youngest person in the school since most of the students were just coming back from the war," John said. "I was exposed to many school organizations, and being young, I had no choice but to keep up."

John's quote in the McGill yearbook, "Activity is the road to knowledge," reflected an impressive list of activities that encompassed managing football, hockey, golf, and athletics teams and being involved in everything from Scarlet Key to the Freshman Reception Committee and student government. "John was hugely into sports, activities, and organizing," says his niece, Diana Knox. "He later tried to instill in many kids that the social part of university is super important as well. Doing things other than school was key for him. He felt this created a better rounded person."

Dobson had always been skeptical of students who are at the top of the class. In his view, real-life experience and good wits, as opposed to academic prowess, were the true measure of a person's abilities, especially in terms of entrepreneurship. This prompted Robert Scully, host of PBS's long-running *The Dobson Series*, in which he interviews leading entrepreneurs, to pen a little poem on the occasion of Dobson's eightieth birthday in 2008. It included the following verse:

John doesn't go for students who are top of the class
All this summa cum laude stuff he finds a bit crass
Tell him in boarding school you were kicked out on your ass
And you'll be his friend for life, he'll give you a free pass.

CHAPTER 3

The "Real World"

*We took this approach: If you came from Mars,
how would you invest in the rest of the world
aside from Canada?*

— JOHN W. DOBSON

Dobson graduated from McGill in 1949 with a bachelor of commerce degree and immediately applied to Harvard Business School's prestigious MBA program. Its case method of teaching approach was quite different from almost anything available in Canada. Dobson was just twenty years old, but he was overflowing with confidence. "I was a proven leader, so it never occurred to me I wouldn't get in," he said. He was wrong. Harvard's dean told him that he was too young and should stay away from university for a year or two and accumulate some work experience. "I thought I'd spend time with my dad at the bank and see the real world. But he told me that wasn't the real world. So I ended up working in a small paint company for a year, selling and mixing paint: the real world!" The experience would serve him well, giving him first-hand exposure to sales and marketing. "Most people don't know the real world until much later in life. I always looked at how I was different from others, and it was because I was ordered to go into the real world by Harvard."

Returning to Harvard a year later, Dobson still found himself the youngest in his class – many of the students had delayed their studies because they had served in the Armed Forces during the Second World War. The ever-energetic Dobson threw himself into the grind of classes and rigorous assignments. "They had case studies," he recalled, "and you had to hand in your work Saturday night at 9:00 p.m. It was all work and no play!"

Yet every spring and fall, Dobson would take time out to stay with new friends and fellow golf aficionados such as Nancy Walker Bush, the sister of the future US President George H.W. Bush, at their home in Concord, Massachusetts. "She was a great, bright girl," he said. "I met lots of people like her while at Harvard and created a large information network, which helped Formula Growth tremendously in later years. In fact, we had a network second to none, and much of that was developed while I was at Harvard. There is nothing like bouncing investment ideas off like-minded investors who have local knowledge."

Dobson graduated from Harvard in 1952 and immediately returned to Montreal. At that time, Harvard MBA graduates had extraordinary opportunities because North America had embarked on its huge post-war expansion, and many companies were in desperate need of young management talent. A degree from Harvard Business School had tremendous cachet and was seen as a ticket to the big time. Prominent Montreal money manager Stephen Jarislowsky, who graduated from Harvard three years before Dobson, notes that seven of his classmates went on to lead Fortune 500 companies.

⊰ DOMINION ENGINEERING WORKS ⊱

Dobson's early ambitions were more modest. His first job was as assistant to Hubert Welsford, president of Dominion Engineering Works, a venerable Montreal manufacturer of electric turbines and paper-making machinery. "The president wanted a business school guy in the mix, and I was that guy," Dobson explained. He stayed at the company for seven years, working at the beck and call of Welsford in a busy office environment. For an ambitious young MBA graduate, it felt like an eternity.

While at Dominion, Dobson demonstrated his skill at judging people's strengths by singling out a junior staffer, Alan Durrell, for promotion. "My dad used to be the first one in the office and the last one out, and John picked up on this," says Durrell's daughter, Nancy Durrell McKenna. "John mentioned to the president that my dad had a great work ethic and should be in line for promotion." Thanks to Dobson, Durrell rose through the ranks at Dominion, and Dobson would become a lifelong friend of the entire Durrell clan. "I remember as a little girl, I'd be excited that Mr Dobson would be coming for dinner," says Nancy, who became Dobson's unofficial goddaughter. "We always referred to him as 'The Dobber.'"

A native of Ottawa, Alan Durrell had been only fourteen years old when his father died. He looked after his mother and four sisters, so there was not a lot of money to go around. "He never went to university and was a self-made man," says Nancy Durrell McKenna. "John has a lot of respect for people with a 'get-up-and-go' attitude, and it was wonderful to see the mutual respect he and my father had for each other. They were on opposite sides of the spectrum in terms of wealth and privilege, but they still had the same values."

Nancy's brother, Jim Durrell, the former mayor of Ottawa, remembers meeting Dobson as a teenager. "He was kind of the family mentor. My father had an enormous respect for him, and we were the same, growing up. He was well educated and had an opinion on everything. And you knew exactly where he stood."

It was while working at Dominion Engineering that Dobson and a number of Harvard alumni and other executives began teaching the Harvard business case method at evening classes organized by Montreal's Junior Board of Trade. That course, with its emphasis on teaching business skills and modern management practices, was to become the foundation for the McGill Executive Development Institute, where Dobson taught for twenty years. "I always believed that universities needed to get more involved in fostering entrepreneurship through specialized programs," Dobson explained. "I especially admired the Harvard model, which had professors of entrepreneurship, and I felt it should be more prevalent in Canada."

One of the directors of the Junior Board of Trade program was William Turner, who had first met Dobson at Harvard Business School and found him to be very gung-ho. "He was a good athlete, liked people, had an infectious attitude, and was very outgoing."

Turner ended up in Montreal through a circuitous route. Born in Pennsylvania of Canadian parents, Turner graduated from Harvard and immediately went to work for Jeep in Toledo, Ohio. "It was the third largest exporter of automobiles after the war because the road system was a mess, and Jeeps were handy in bad road conditions. After two years in Toledo, they wanted to send me to Africa to work at a supply depot there, but I was married and had a child on the way, so I quit and went to work for Ingersoll-Rand with another Harvard classmate." Turner later joined Power Corporation of Canada in Montreal and became CFO of its subsidiary, Bathurst Paper. He stayed there for twenty years, overseeing the merger with Consolidated Paper in 1966, which created Consolidated-Bathurst Inc., where Turner became CEO and a leader of Canada's pulp and paper industry.

When he first moved to Montreal, William Turner recalls bumping into Dobson, who was already "mixed up" in the Executive Development Institute and active with the Junior Board of Trade. "He and his buddies had gone down to Harvard and asked for some business cases," he recalls. Dobson asked him whether he was willing to do some teaching. Turner agreed and ended up lecturing at the institute for more than ten years. He notes that in the 1950s, there were not many Canadians in business school, and few Canadian universities offered an MBA (the University of Western Ontario had started its program in 1948). This made the program developed by Dobson and his friends particularly timely. "No Canadian university of the day appreciated the pluses of business education," he says. "McGill regarded a commerce degree as a good preparation for becoming a civil servant in Ottawa. We were involved in teaching cases for more than a decade, and McGill then took this work over and finally expanded its commerce department into a wider mission."

Willard Ellis, former executive director of the Executive Development Institute, remembers Dobson as a valued yet underpaid lecturer. "We always got a chuckle out of the fact that I paid him the magnanimous sum of $20 an hour for his efforts," he wrote on the occasion of Dobson's eightieth birthday in 2008. "John's support of many activities and individuals is well known, but if the true story of the full extent was ever actually known, they would be equalled by few, if any, in Canada. His kindness and thoughtfulness knew no bounds."

In his 1997 induction as a member of the Order of Canada, Dobson's work as an educator was cited: "He also conceived and co-founded the Executive Development Institute at McGill University. As a result of his initiative, the Institute merged with the Montreal Board of Trade to form the Management Institute, which has had a positive impact on the Business Administration program, bringing students and business people together in a dynamic learning environment."

Robert Paterson, who joined the Royal Bank after graduating in commerce from McGill, remembers getting together informally with Dobson and other young members of Montreal's business community every two weeks to discuss Harvard case studies. Since many were still living at home, they would often meet at their parents' houses. "We enjoyed getting into their liquor cabinets at the end of the evening." After a year and a half of discussing case studies and business practices, the group organized a "fathers' luncheon" to thank them for their hospitality. "I organized one at a private club on Sherbrooke Street East, away from the group's traditional Anglo-Montreal haunts," recalls Paterson. "This was novel for people who would never have set foot in the place. It was the headquarters of the Liberal Party. Sydney Dobson got up and thanked us for our hospitality and said he hoped we had a great future with all our advantages. Lorne Webster got up and said, 'I was always told I was born with a silver spoon in my mouth – but it's still tougher than you think.'"

Dobson and several other members of the study group would soon go on to form a unique investment club that would put their new-found business acumen to the test.

⤳ A FORMULA FOR GROWTH ⤳

Dobson's early silica mining investment debacle, in which he lost all the money set aside for him by his father, did nothing to dampen his interest in the stock market. Nor did it shake his optimism about the benefits that could be reaped with the right approach to investing. In the fall of 1959, he left Dominion Engineering to work as an economist for the Montreal brokerage firm of C.J. Hodgson. Soon after joining Hodgson, Dobson began to consider setting up an informal investment club, and he discussed the possibility with two close friends, John Rook and Walter Cottingham. Rook was general manager of Power Corporation of Canada, where Dobson's good friend Bill Turner worked. Cottingham, a member of the wealthy Sherwin Williams family, was a schoolboy friend and fellow McGill alumnus. He was working as assistant-treasurer for Premium Iron Ores in Montreal.

As Cottingham recalls: "It was John's concept. He had gone to Harvard Business School and met a variety of people in the investment business. He had come to the conclusion that Canada represented only 2 per cent of the world economy, and that we should broaden out and invest outside in smaller companics since they were, theoretically, faster growing. He talked it up to me, and he also talked to John Rook and various other people."

The trio had all been looking for new investment opportunities on their own, but they did not find much in Canada that was exciting, Dobson later said. "So we took this approach: 'If you came from Mars, how would you invest in the rest of the world aside from Canada?' The answer: develop a strong network of people who are experts in various countries, and look for high-growth companies around the world."

Dobson, who was just entering his thirties, went about assembling a hand-picked group of investors who could help identify international trends and select investments from a large number of opportunities. By the summer of 1960, the three friends had signed up eight other young men, and together they all agreed to put up a total of $134,000 (over $1 million in today's money) in seed money for an investment club – which was to become Formula Growth Fund.

The investors were a diverse lot, drawn together through common friendships, family ties, or school alliances. By pooling their investment knowledge and backgrounds, they hoped to leverage their individual financial resources while sharing ideas about investment approaches and philosophies. Apart from Dobson, John Rook, and Walter Cottingham, who each put in $20,000, the group included a who's who of current and would-be members of Montreal's elite. They included people who would in the future become federal and provincial cabinet ministers, financial titans, and even a prime minister.

Among the pioneering investors was John Turner, then an up-and-coming lawyer at Stikeman Elliott in Montreal. Elected as a Montreal MP in 1962, he would later serve as the seventeenth prime minister of Canada. Turner first met Dobson in St Andrews, New Brunswick, at the age of about sixteen, while he was vacationing at the home of his mother and stepfather. (The Dobsons used to stay in cottages behind the iconic Algonquin Hotel in St Andrews by-the-Sea.) "I spent part of every summer there for years, except for when I was in Oxford, and we used to play golf together," says Turner. "John and I hit it off right away and were friends since 1945." The two went on to see each other regularly in Montreal during the 1950s when Turner started practising law. "He asked me to incorporate Formula Growth in 1960, and I became its first secretary."

Also on board was Lorne Webster, a member of the powerful Webster business family, who would go on to build an empire in insurance, trust, real estate, and investment management. Heward Grafftey, a friend of Dobson's, also jumped in. Grafftey was a businessman who had just been elected Progressive Conservative MP for Brome-Missisquoi riding in Quebec. Frank L. Schnabel, a securities analyst who was working with the Webster family's Imperial Trust Company, signed on, too. Rounding off the group were Dobson friends and investment managers Andy Hugessen, Peter Cross, and Jacques Glorieux. Each would put up $10,000, with the exception of Robert Midgley, a relative of Dobson's. "I had just graduated from McGill Medical School and didn't have that much money," says Midgley, a doctor and plastic surgeon. "You needed $10,000 to get into the fund, and I had nowhere near that, but John let me in for $4,000."

Although Dobson was only in his early thirties and didn't have much of an investment track record, Midgley says he trusted him implicitly. "John was young and aggressive and he said 'why not?' and I said, 'sure!' I never really knew the other investors. I met some, but they were all of different walks of life. I did not attend any of the meetings or anything. I wasn't part of the team because I only contributed $4,000. I was just a poor kid then! I put all my faith in John. I believed in him, and so did my dad." (Based on Formula Growth Fund's historic performance, Midgley's initial investment of $4,000 would have grown by over 600 times, to about $2.4 million)

For Dobson, the investment pool was far from a gamble. "The Quebec silica mine fiasco was a good lesson," he said. "I wasn't aware that I was taking any particular risk. If you have the best network and the best people to invest in running growing companies, it doesn't seem like a gamble. I was confident that the money that I put in was going to accumulate, but I wasn't trying to build a business."

Formula Growth Fund was officially established on 27 June 1960, with initial units being issued for the equivalent of $9 each. (The units were initially priced at $1,000 each. In subsequent years, there were two 10-for-1 splits and a 10 per cent distribution, bringing the adjusted initial value to $9.) The fund began on a very informal basis. Walter Cottingham says, "We all did a bit of a research and talked it up and thought about it. We met perhaps once a month in somebody's house and had a drink and put a portfolio together."

∞ INTERNATIONAL INVESTMENTS ∞

With advice from Peter Cross and contacts in Europe, the members initially bought a basket of stocks in France, Italy, Argentina, Spain, France, and the United States. "We all did stock picking," says Cottingham. "We used our contacts and our investment knowledge to put the portfolios together collectively. We all took a kick at the can with various companies. We agreed. We disagreed. We investigated. We all were there trying to find good companies."

Ian Soutar, a founding partner of investment management firm Pembroke Management and Dobson's advisor and friend for over forty-five years, says the idea from the very start was to invest internationally. "This was novel at the time. Dobson thought everyone was looking at Canada and the United States, not at these greater opportunities abroad." Soutar first met Dobson in the mid-1960s, when he was working in the investment department at Sun Life. They became fast friends. "We agreed on a whole lot of issues," he says. "We both had many of the same views, loved golf, loved the investment business, and loved investing in small companies. That was sort of my background, and that was John's background. It was a natural thing for us."

Japan was a market of special interest for the young investors, and, at one point, the fund had a fifth of its portfolio there. "We did very, very well in the Japan market and reasonably well in the other ones. That was a big bonus," says Walter Cottingham. "Japan was doing extremely well in the early 1960s, and John thought the Japanese were the new business leaders," says money manager Stephen Jarislowsky, who has had a lifelong fascination with Japanese culture (he worked for the US Army in Japan after the Second World War) and was a friend of Dobson's for over sixty years. "Everybody thought it was a Japanese miracle. They were trying to figure out how they did it, how they organized and all of that. John was very smitten with that kind of success."

The group was looking for growth stories in what was to become known as the "Growth Formula." According to this formula, every stock held should be capable of growing at 20 per cent a year. The time span is relatively short. The fund looks for stocks that will be performing well in one year to three years' time. If the 20 per cent target is not met, the stock is sold. If the stock performs well, it is held unless the price/earnings multiple three years out exceeds 25, when the holding is reduced to 1 per cent of the total fund, and eventually sold entirely when the upside is limited. In addition, the holding cannot form more than 7 per cent of the total portfolio. Diversification has always been key.

"My guiding principle was always to shoot for 20 per cent performance for our unit holders, which includes ourselves," said Dobson. "Everything else was secondary. Making money on stocks was the game, not management fees. We also wanted to always have fun doing it because you can't last in this business if you can't have fun. Excluding some exceptions, we invested by targeting 20 per cent earnings per share (EPS) growth, 20 per cent sales growth, and 20 per cent return on equity."

⊙ EARLY INTEREST IN THE FUND ⊙

The fund was an immediate success, rising 19.1 per cent between 1 July and 31 December 1960 and climbing 56.4 per cent by 31 December 1961 to $204.29 a unit from a pre-split $100. Word of this lucrative little fund quickly got around the small Montreal investment community. Friends and business associates clamoured to get on board, many of them Dobson's fellow golfers at Mount Bruno on Montreal's South Shore. They included the following:

- The Birks family, owners of the legendary jewellery chain known for its famous blue boxes. "I became involved because of my respect for John Dobson," says G. Drummond (Drummie) Birks, son of company founder, Henry Birks. "I thought he was an able investor. I knew him socially as well and always had enjoyed his company. Our fathers went way back, too. I remember playing golf with both our fathers in the 1930s, when I was a junior member of Bruno."

- Hugh Hallward, head of Argo Construction, who later took John Rook's place as a director of Formula Growth Limited. He was a founding investor in the Montreal Expos baseball club in 1968, alongside Charles Bronfman and others. "I went to school with John and Walter at Selwyn House, and we used to play sports together," said Hallward. "I knew all the players, and although I had my own investments, I thought Formula Growth had an interesting approach. We had meetings and occasionally arguments one way or the other about certain investments, but by and large, there was a convivial consensus." Hallward died in August 2013, a few weeks after his old friend John Dobson.

- Neil Ivory, a portfolio manager at Arbuckle, Govett & Co. Ltd. (dissolved in 1976), who in 1968 would co-found Pembroke Management, manager of the highly regarded GBC family of mutual funds, along with Clifford L. Larock, Scott Taylor, and Ian Soutar. Pembroke and its partners would be long-time investors and trusted advisors to Formula Growth for many decades.

- Donald Johnston, a lawyer at Heenan Blaikie, who would become a member of the cabinet of Prime Minister Pierre Trudeau and later Secretary-General of the Organisation for Economic Co-operation and Development (OECD). He also acted as Formula Growth's second company secretary. "I was conscripted by John Turner when I graduated from law school in 1958," Johnston recalls. "I was an articling student and worked closely with Turner and his clients and friends. One of them was this group of guys, who were the nucleus of Formula Growth: John Dobson, Walter Cottingham, etc. I took over the files in 1962 and became the lawyer for Formula Growth, and we restructured as a management company at that time. It was run by John and Walter at that point. I went to the meetings and got to know the guys pretty well. We remained friends. I was the lawyer and secretary and kept the books."

Also among the early investors were investment advisor Bobby Hall, Dick Forest (later an executive at Air Canada), boyhood friend Jacques Tétrault, and Nassie Godel, who had met Dobson while working at C.J. Hodgson and was a fellow golf fanatic. "People became interested," says Walter Cottingham. "I don't think we hustled it, but we did invite people to come in because they had some money and contacts. They were keen about the idea and the concept. They knew John and all of us. So it grew from a private group that met once a month into a growing business. It was good to have them on board."

The fund grew so quickly that by 1962, Dobson, John Rook and Walter Cottingham decided to leave their day jobs to devote their full time efforts to the venture. Cottingham stayed on as a consultant to Premium Iron Ore, and they all moved into his small office. Together, the trio then owned about 20 per cent of the units of the fund and were therefore focused on ensuring its success.

"The office was slightly crowded, but the fund was growing," says Walter Cottingham. "I know John had the idea that it shouldn't become too big, and I don't know if in his mind too big was $15 million or $30 million. We got up to our target over a period of time. It was stimulating and an interesting concept that forced people away from investing in big companies and into small companies that grew quicker. It was original."

While relying mainly on contacts in target countries, the trio also began travelling to visit companies that had investment potential.

Dobson and Ian Soutar went to Japan initially, followed by Walter Cottingham and Peter Cross. "Even back then, John liked to travel with his golf clubs. He would take them with him when visiting companies and brokers," says Cottingham. "Over the years, we cultivated a fair number of brokers and advisors in the United States and in Europe to come up with ideas."

Dobson travelled around the world in 1963, more for pleasure than for business. During a trip to Japan with Ian Soutar about six years later, he had an experience that underscored, he later said, the role luck always played in his life. "I arrived in Honolulu a day before Soutar, and the hotel misspelled my name in the registry. When Ian arrived the next day to check in, they said they had no record of me being there. He didn't know where to go or what to do, so he took a walk on the beach. I was also walking on the beach and out of sheer luck, I ran into him. If that hadn't happened, the entire trip would have been a disaster." Dobson was a big advocate of the idea that luck is an essential part of both life and investing. Sometimes you simply need to show up.

⚭ UPS AND DOWNS ⚭

Looking for quick-growing companies with aggressive business plans has usually pointed Formula Growth Fund to invest in small- and medium-cap growth stocks. As a result, its performance is subject to a high degree of volatility. Like most investment portfolios, it has also been buffeted by periodic stock market dips over its more than half-century of existence.

The first occurred soon after its foundation, when the Cuban missile crisis sent the Dow Jones Industrial Average into a downspin. The Dow dropped 26.5 per cent from its height of 728.8 on 1 December 1961, a year after the election of President John F. Kennedy, to a low of 535.76 on 26 June 1962. Tensions were heightened in October 1962, and the Dow dropped 2 per cent the day after President Kennedy's famous speech warning the Russians to withdraw missiles from Cuba. The Standard & Poor's 500 fell nearly 28 per cent during the same mini-bear market.

The main culprits for the stock market dips were fears surrounding the Cold War, the failed Bay of Pigs invasion, the Cuban missile crisis, and the threat of nuclear attack. The blame cannot be laid on the economy, which was poised to begin a decade-long expansion. Even though it was not fully invested in the US market, as it would be in later years, Formula Growth Fund units fell nearly 29 per cent during the mini-bear market of 1962. But they recovered in 1963, climbing nearly 17 per cent, and were up 7 per cent and 51 per cent in 1964 and 1965, respectively, establishing their historical trajectory: up and to the right.

CHAPTER 4

Triumphs and Turmoil

[Dobson] never worried about the downside; he
always looked to the upside. But there were a lot of
people saying "Gosh, what the heck are you doing
with my money?"

— IAN SOUTAR

Despite the hiccup of 1962 when Formula Growth Fund units fell by nearly a third, the early days of the Fund proved to be fabulously rewarding for unit holders. A buoyant stock market and astute investment decisions by Dobson and his colleagues resulted in excellent returns. By the end of 1965, just five years after the founding of the Fund, its unit value had jumped by 151 per cent, which was triple the 51.35 per cent gain for the Dow Jones Industrial Average. Formula Growth Fund was still small and closely held, with 123 registered owners owning a total of 11,135 units valued at $1,772,940. The directors of the Fund's management firm and their families themselves owned 27.3 per cent of the units.

But after that initial exuberance, the following decade proved trying for investors' patience. Gains turned into losses, leading to a nasty battle that almost resulted in the ouster of John Dobson and the souring of some of the close friendships that had been at the heart of Formula Growth Fund.

After an early interest in a broad range of overseas investments, notably in the emerging Japanese economy, Dobson would ultimately decide to stick closer to home, namely the growing US market. By the end of 1965, a dominant part of Formula Growth Fund's portfolio already consisted of US stocks, although the Fund would continue to return to Japanese and other markets in varying degrees in the sub-sequent decade. There were only four Canadian companies in the list and just one outside North America – Sagimo, a French property firm. The Fund's US holdings ranged from Tektronix Inc. (an emerging technology firm that had its IPO in 1963) and Swank Inc. (a maker of costume jewellery) to companies such as United Airlines and Pennsylvania Railroad, which were still of modest enough size to meet Dobson's investment criteria.

Formula Growth Fund was also beginning to evolve into a more formal business, despite Dobson's desire to keep it as an overgrown investment club. In 1965, the company was still being run by a group of friends and associates, most of whom had been around since the initial days. The officers and directors at the time were John Dobson, president; Walter Cottingham, vice-president and treasurer; Frank Schnabel, vice-president of research; Lorne Webster, vice-president; Drummond Birks, director; Hugh Hallward, director; Neil Ivory, director; and Donald Johnston, secretary.

As Ian Soutar notes, "I think a lot of people in the business tried to make their money by making the assets under management grow through marketing techniques. But John was never interested in that at all. He was interested in making money for the unit holders and investors in the Fund, but he wasn't going to make money off the Fund by the fees that were coming in. The Fund did grow a lot, and after a period of time, there were fees coming in, which you need to pay the people working. But it was really his objective at all times to just make money for the investors or create wealth through capital gains. He never wanted to make money off the investors."

In the early years, the total management fee of the fund started at 2 per cent on the first $2 million of assets and slid down to 1 per cent for assets under management over $10 million. Strangely, this sliding scale dropped to 0.75 per cent at $100 million of assets, at a time when getting to $100 million in assets was still considered unachievable. Yet, with the power of compounding, the assets soon grew to well over $100 million, and the 0.75 per cent fee kicked in. (The fee was applied equally to all unit holders, regardless of the size of their investments.) Because the expenses of running the firm had escalated over the years, Formula Growth Fund simplified the fee structure in the 1990s to a 1 per cent flat fee, still unusually low by industry standards. In contrast, a shareholder in a mutual fund can pay as much as 5 to 8 per cent in front-end loads that go to brokers and intermediaries, as well as 2– 3 per cent per year in management fees, known as the MER (management expense ratio).

Dobson and his colleagues also wanted to avoid building a big fund because they felt it would be difficult to successfully invest large sums of money. As proof, they cited the mediocre performance of most professionally managed funds compared to the performance of various stocks. A large fund, they observed, tends to go up and down like the stock market as a whole because it lacks the flexibility to move large amounts of shares as investment conditions change.

The decade that followed the initial golden years would be momentous for Formula Growth Fund, as North American stock markets were rocked by such events as the Vietnam War, the Watergate scandal, and the 1973 oil embargo. There would be a significant expansion of the Fund's investment network, key staff additions and, in the most serious threat to the Fund's survival, an attempt to oust Dobson from the Fund's management.

In 1972, Walter Cottingham decided he wanted to broaden his horizons. He decamped for London, then an emerging financial centre, to work for an offshore fund called Eagle Investments, which had a loose affiliation with Formula Growth. "I was still working with Formula and coming back to pass on or receive ideas from them." He returned to Canada two years later, but he left Formula Growth Fund for good to work with another Montreal investment management firm. "By then, Formula Growth had sold most of its overseas portfolio to focus solely on US companies. They discovered that their research time and limited resources would be best served by investing only in small-growth companies in the US," Cottingham notes.

Ian Soutar remembers going to Japan with Dobson in 1969 to investigate stock prospects there, but by the mid-1970s, all Japanese stocks in the firm's portfolio had been sold. "My partner Neil Ivory, an early investor in Formula Growth Fund, advised John to stick closer to home, to focus on the US market, and this influenced John's decision. He saw that there were lots of opportunities in the United States."

Randall Kelly, who would join Formula Growth Fund in 1984, at the age of 27, and become its president in 1992, notes that Dobson often complained that he left Japan too early. But in hindsight, it was shown to be the right thing to do. "There is no doubt that the Japanese stock market was on fire during the 1980s, but it became a bubble of epic proportions in the 1990s and beyond," he says. "The market has since been moored in muck for decades and has produced a negative return for twenty-five years. Many Japanese companies made for questionable investments," Kelly adds. "They didn't have a high return on equity. They didn't pay attention to growing earnings. They had these lifetime pacts with their employees. The Japanese economy didn't have the healthy obsolescence you see in the United States, where old, tired companies perish and new vibrant ones are born. Free market forces just weren't evident to me. Companies there didn't make sense. And to top it off, accounting practices were often flakey."

Dobson said he decided to abandon Japan for a number of reasons. "First of all, it was too far flung, and the objective of Formula Growth has always been to have people on the ground in the area to find good ideas. That was virtually impossible to do in Japan with such a small staff. Second, we wanted to bring something different to Canadians than what they could get in Montreal or elsewhere in Canada. We wanted to narrow it down to the United States alone and use our expertise and network there to the greatest effect."

Investable Companies

By the mid- to late 1970s, Formula Growth Fund would focus almost exclusively on the United States markets, and it continues to do so today. "We like the American market because it offers an almost infinite amount of ways to play all sorts of different businesses," explained John Dobson. "These same US companies give you worldwide exposure, and many of them operate with big international businesses. So you can get international bang for the buck by buying US-listed stocks. We like to focus on growth stocks or companies that grow their earnings quickly. We want stocks that can grow their earnings per share at above the average rates, and we like to pay below average multiples for these above average rates of growth."

It is tricky to find these aggressive growth stocks, Dobson acknowledged. "You have to beat the bushes to find them." They can be either newly emerging growth stocks that come out of initial public offerings, or they can be companies that are re-emerging with a new product, new management, or a new business line. "The trick for us is to determine whether the story is believable, whether it's going to happen as scripted, and we need to be in front of the story early so we are there before the Street is aware of the idea." Formula Growth Fund often bet against some of the skepticism that normally surrounds growth stocks, Dobson noted. "You have to be careful, as many growth business plans don't come true. In order to help our batting average, we do a lot of kicking of the tires."

While there are thousands of public companies in the United States, Formula Growth Fund president Randy Kelly notes that perhaps half are not really investable because they are dollar stocks, companies losing lots of money, or companies with market caps that are too small. "On the other hand, there are probably 3,000 or 4,000 stocks that are investable. At any one moment, we are looking at all of those stocks. We comb through them to find the 100 or so that might form a portfolio for us."

There is never a shortage of good ideas to invest in, Kelly adds. Because Formula Growth has been in business for over fifty years, it has a very deep database on many of the investable companies in the United States that it can cull from. Additionally, it deals with 100 different brokers on the sell side – from the largest all the way down to regional brokers who might be located in Minneapolis or Little Rock, far away from New York. "It is important to talk to everyone, as you never know where the next great stock will come from."

Because the fund has been in business so long, it has a very large buy-side network of friends and peers that it talks to. "These are people with whom we compete, I suppose, but for the most part, it's really just friendly competition," says Randy Kelly. "It is quite a fraternity among the people who buy growth stocks. We share ideas and trade information with our peers on the buy side as long as it is a two-way street. All of these ways form the basis for our idea flow. Essentially, Formula has a tremendous information network that allows us to get quickly to the bottom line of a story."

Currently, Formula Growth Fund has an in-house team that does nothing but research, model and screen for stocks, and talk to management teams in order to discern whether or not the stock is a good investment for the Fund. Team members also spend a lot of time on the road visiting company headquarters.

In the early 1970s, Paul Levesque, an investment banker based in New York City who had worked with Dobson and Formula Growth for several years, suggested that Dobson call a bright young analyst at Commercial Trust named Peter Mackechnie to help lead the Fund's aggressive expansion into the US stock market. "John phoned me and said, 'I've heard good things about you from Paul Levesque and Charlie Baillie (then head of the TD Bank),'" recalls Mackechnie.

In 1972, Mackechnie was offered a position as executive vice-president. He took the job right away, thankful to get away from the bureaucracy of Commercial Trust. "Formula Growth was a wide-open-type thing, where you just talked to John Dobson about his thoughts, about looking at certain companies. And he was always very good and excited about it. He trusted people's judgments, let them take risks."

∞ TARGET SHEETS ∞

Peter Mackechnie was particularly impressed by Dobson's use of what he called "target sheets." He would look at the names and the numbers on the target sheets, and if they were very promising, relative to everything else, he would give the okay and tell Mackechnie to see what he could chase down.

Formula Growth Fund has employed potential or target sheets for half a century. The target sheets are customized spread sheets to assess stocks. In addition to an initial evaluation prior to purchase, target sheets are also used to track a stock's ongoing performance.

"We manage the portfolio with very strict price targets and very tight qualitative scripts or stories associated with each stock," explains Randy Kelly. "If a management team tells us they are going to do ABC and they do XYZ, we're going to sell the stock. We model everything we own. If we expect the company to earn $0.10 in a quarter and it earns only $0.06, then we are going to be very strict about why the company missed the EPS target and likely sell the stock."

To control risk, Formula Growth Fund also runs with very tight stops to protect the downside. (A stop is an order to buy or sell a security when its price surpasses a particular point, thus ensuring a greater probability of achieving a predetermined entry or exit price.) "If a stock price moves down and we don't quite understand it, we are going to sell the stock and ask questions later," says Randy Kelly. "On the other hand, if a company is successful and hits our upside price targets based on our modelling, we are also very strict about selling. To manage money successfully, you have to have a tough-sell discipline. You have to stick to your disciplines, and it's one of the key features of Formula Growth."

∞ DOBSON DINNERS ∞

Peter Mackechnie had experience covering hotel and restaurant stocks in the United States, so he promptly started looking for opportunities for Formula Growth Fund in California and the Western United States. "These regions hadn't been particularly high on Dobson's list, but after we got out there several times, he saw that the companies were dynamic and fast-growing," says Mackechnie.

Mackechnie and Dobson would attend investment conferences in California and elsewhere regularly and cultivated a network of fund managers and brokers who would prove invaluable sources of advice. They also launched an annual investment banquet in San Francisco that would famously become known as "the Dobson Dinners." At each of these events, participants would pick a stock they thought would be the best performer in the coming year, and a friendly competition ensued. "Many of these people would be out west for an investment conference, such as one organized by Hambrecht & Quist [a San Francisco-based investment bank], and we would steal them away for our dinner," said Dobson. "It was all part of our strategy of building the best information network around."

Peter Mackechnie was in charge of keeping statistics about winners and losers for nearly twenty-five years. "I calculated who was winning beforehand and then showed up at the dinner with who owed what to whom and that kind of thing," Mackechnie says. In fact, he continued to act as master of ceremonies at the dinners for many years, even after he left Formula Growth Fund.

The Dobson Dinners were lavish affairs, usually held at the San Francisco Yacht Club and attended by thirty-five or forty people. "People just didn't want to stop coming, and participants were called Dobson Dinner Players," says Mackechnie. "We had some very good guys: Tom Bailey way back in the early years, who made his billions in Denver; Phil Hempleman was also there. He went on to make a huge fortune in stocks. (In 1987, Hempleman founded Connecticut-based Ardsley Partners, a long/short equity hedge fund with approximately $1 billion under management in 2012.) He came for many years, and it annoyed him that he could make many millions doing what he did in stock funds, but he could not pick a winning stock in the Dobson Dinners." To the bemusement, or annoyance, of many Dobson Dinner Players, pride of place often went to representatives of tiny Formula Growth Fund, which won a disproportionate amount of the time since they were such great stock pickers. Randy Kelly alone won five times.

Ted Ashford, a US portfolio manager known as the "Delaware Dynamo," who was featured in John Train's 1994 book *The Money Masters*, attended the dinners for many years. "It started as a few people going to dinner and picking a long [buy] and a short [sell]. You'd come back a year later and figure out who won," says Ashford, a long-time friend of Dobson's. "Peter [Mackechnie] would talk about the worst first, and the guy with the worst long had to pay the guy with the best long. The same system was used for the shorts. And Peter would just roast the losers! These were bright people, but they got an earful," Ashford chuckles.

Peter Mackechnie also attended a similar event organized by Dobson in New York that was dubbed the "20 Per Centers." This brought together like-minded growth-stock investors, including legendary investor Sir John Templeton. "The people at that event were just beyond smart," Mackechnie says. "They were just great analysts or money managers, and it was all because of Dobson just being creative enough to seek these guys out and pick their brains. That was his real forte."

Ted Ashford clearly remembers his first "20 Per Centers" dinner. "Templeton was sitting on my left. John called the meeting to order and asked Templeton to start off and share his thoughts. He covered everything I had planned to cover, and I was next in line. Everyone laughed, because I had nothing left to say!"

Ian Soutar says it is remarkable how a relatively small money manager in Montreal was able to find its way into the biggest and most successful money management firms and conferences and attract heavy hitters to its events. "It was John's initiative to get activities like the Dobson Dinner and the 20 Per Centers going. It was a brilliant idea because I think those relationships really helped in terms of the Fund's performance. It was a lot of fun, and John would always pick up the tab for this stuff. Participants enjoyed meeting other people doing the same kind of things, and John was able to attract some of the best talent in America to his events. So it was something everybody felt was really important to attend because they were brushing shoulders with people who were good for business. And, although there were other great conferences, and these people had choices, they would always come to the Dobson Dinners. It was the thing to do."

Another critical player in Formula Growth's success joined the organization in those heady days of the early 1970s, although initially only part-time. Bette Lou Reade would play a key role in the Fund's growth for nearly forty years. Reade had met Dobson at McGill, where she had spent two years in accounting before switching to arts. "Friends of mine were friends of his, but I didn't really get to know him well," she recalls. Reade was in the midst of a divorce and in difficult financial straits when she was hired by Formula Growth to come in two days a week to do the books in the tough early 1970s. "The only other person there was Peter Mackechnie. We were at 666 Sherbrooke Street West, and it was a measly little office. We didn't have a whole bunch of money under management, and it got smaller."

Reade's accounting work started in 1973, and for the next two years, she never prepared an "up" monthly portfolio valuation – for twenty-four months in a row!

Formula Unit Trust

In February 1976, Peter Mackechnie was instrumental in setting up Formula Unit Trust, Formula Growth's institutional fund that mirrored Formula Growth Fund and would thrive for over three decades. It peaked at about $500 million (US) in size and returned 11.7 per cent (compound annual growth rate – CAGR) versus 8.2 per cent (without dividends) and 11.6 per cent (with dividends) for the Standard & Poor's 500 over thirty-two years.

The idea stemmed from Dobson's and Mackechnie's frequent travels to the United States, where they met contacts who had a lot of institutional clients. They decided it was worth taking a shot at the institutions because Dobson had such a fabulous long track record with Formula Growth. Even though the Fund had suffered a couple of dismal years in 1973 and 1974, it had jumped over 70 per cent in 1975, making it a good time to offer institutions exposure to small- and mid-cap US companies and to the US dollar. "John felt that everyone should have some portion of their money in companies that grew 20 per cent or better because he genuinely believed that if the company grew at 20 per cent a year, then the stocks would grow 20 per cent and so would your portfolio," explains Mackechnie. "Compounding wise, that was just a huge number, so a lot of people bought into that."

One of the first investors was the Birks family, who put a portion of the family's Foundation money in Formula Unit Trust. Then the Royal Bank and Air Canada came on board, seeking exposure to the US growth sector for their pension funds.

Peter Mackechnie recalls that he and Dobson were having lunch one day at the St James Club in Montreal with Tim DeWolf, then pension fund general manager at Air Canada. "I can never forget that one because at the end of the lunch, DeWolf said they were going to invest $2 million in Formula Unit Trust. Dobson coughed and choked and his onion soup went all over the table. What a tremendous shock we both had! Fortunately, I had nothing in my mouth, but I almost choked because we just kept thinking of what the management fee on the $2 million would give. It was big money in those days, and with the Formula Growth Fund losing business, we needed it to help pay for our overhead."

At one time, Formula Unit Trust boasted an impressive list of institutional investors, including Northern Electric (later Nortel), Bimcor, University of Toronto, McGill University, Ontario Hydro, CP, Montreal Trust, and Consolidated-Bathurst. However, by 2008, Randy Kelly decided to wrap up the Trust after all but two of the investors – McGill and Air Canada – had left. "Our 1 per cent fee was no longer attractive for them, and there were other alternatives such as exchange traded funds (ETFs)." Adds Formula Growth executive René Catafago, "Our small-to-mid-cap approach no longer suited them very well. Plus, they did not enjoy the joint meetings and sharing of information among each other." Air Canada and McGill agreed to move their portfolios to Formula Growth's hedge fund platform, launched in 2002, and McGill remains an investor to this day.

∞ ATTEMPTED PALACE COUP ∞

Formula Growth Fund's poor performance in the early 1970s provoked questions about Dobson's unwillingness to sell losing stocks. Ultimately, this led to an attempt by some unit holders and directors to force him out.

"The market went down enormously from 1968 to 1974, especially in the kind of stocks Formula Growth was investing in," recalls Ian Soutar. "The years 1973 and 1974 – following the Yom Kippur War and the formation of a strong OPEC cartel – were especially awful periods of time. And I would imagine that not only did the Fund go down a lot, but the economics of the Fund must have been really struggling."

Formula CFO René Catafago notes that in 1974, when the whole world was "anti-stock" – everyone was shying away from the stock market – Formula Growth generated only about $75,000 in revenues from fees. "The year 1974 was a disaster of enormous proportions. The net asset value of Formula Growth went down every month for two years. So we were really on the verge of death."

This caused a huge strain, not only financially, but within Formula Growth's tightly knit group of directors and investors. "There were clearly divisions in terms of the 'right kind' of investment policy for the firm at that time," says Ian Soutar. "Dobson had a philosophy of finding good growth companies and hanging on to them. He never worried about the downside; he always looked to the upside. But there were a lot of people saying 'Gosh, what the heck are you doing with my money?' The unit value had gone down hugely, and many people were telling John he was crazy. You've got to realize that stocks that go up could go down. Everyone was saying Dobson's clearly lost it."

Walter Cottingham acknowledged that he was extremely frustrated with Dobson's reluctance to sell losers. "John was most optimistic at market bottoms, and he would say the stocks were just too cheap, and a lot of other people would say the stocks were worthless, that they should be tossed and cash should be raised. But John just felt they were too cheap. He was a great optimist." The reality was that Dobson was usually right; stocks may drop sharply, but over time, they would always roar back!

McGill Professor Reuven Brenner, a long-time associate of Dobson's and occasional advisor to the Formula Growth team, argues today that Dobson's optimism was a big factor behind his success. "In the financial sector, optimism is a must since it exists to finance the future, among others, by correcting mispricing," Brenner says. "If you expect the end of the world, there is no scope for finance. Of course, timing matters. But if you finance entrepreneurial, small, but growing firms, you must be an optimist. You must believe that the United States would eventually correct the mistakes that have been compounding. And sooner rather than later."

Brenner says Dobson always had confidence that markets can weather even the worst storms, a sunny viewpoint that Brenner did not always share. "He had a more idealistic view of markets and what could be done than I have. John thought that things could be solved very quickly. I believe bankruptcy is the mother of invention – and until you get there, all those in power, and fearing losing it, will do everything they can to correct the grave mistakes they made. We differed on the speed at which things can be done. I spent the first fourteen years of my life in Romania under Communism and knew that there were no Communists there. Just politicians, apparatchiks, and opportunists doing all they could to get in power and keep themselves there. Most politicians, bureaucracies, and all those depending on government for handouts in the West are no different. In politics, as in business, fear of default is the mother of invention. Only in business and in the West, we have far more ways to correct the mistakes faster."

Pessimism about the market was so rife in the mid-1970s that one of Formula Growth's clients, Harris Silver, came into the office one day and explained he planned to liquidate his holdings in the Fund and all his other stocks and buy gold with the proceeds. Peter Mackechnie recalls, "He said he was putting the gold in a safety deposit box, and every time he bought goods or services, he planned to pay for them by shaving off pieces of gold, sort of a bartering type of thing."

Scott Taylor, Ian Soutar's partner at Pembroke Management, a long-time director of Formula Growth and a friend of Dobson's, remembers how Walter Cottingham and Dobson started to drift apart. Tensions were also high with Lorne Webster. "People on the board had to intercede to make sure Dobson would take control and move things forward. I was present at the time, but not involved – just aware of the stresses that were present." To add to the tension in the office, Peter Mackechnie was a heavy smoker, a habit that Dobson detested. "He was always on Peter's back about smoking," says Bette Lou Reade. "So eventually, Peter used to leave the office every half hour or so to have a cigarette. That also became a matter of great discussion."

There was good reason for the investor unhappiness. In just one year, between September 1973 and September 1974, the per-unit value of Formula Growth plunged by nearly 50 per cent, to $240.61, compared with a drop of 33 per cent in the TSX and 36 per cent in the Dow Jones Industrial Average (DJIA). Total assets totalled just $4.9 million. But for those who had been with Formula Growth Fund from the start in 1960, fund units were still up 167 per cent compared with a gain of 52 per cent for the TSX and a decline of 5 per cent for the DJIA. Between 1972 and 1974, the US economy went from an annual growth rate of 7.2 per cent to a decline of 2.1 per cent. Oil jumped 70 per cent, from $3 a barrel to $5.11 a barrel, beginning with the October 1973 OPEC oil embargo. Inflation also emerged as a major concern, and interest rates were about to soar.

In October of 1974, an unusually defensive Dobson wrote a sombre letter to unit holders, acknowledging that he may have underestimated the severity of the market downturn. "For the past two years, we have given you various reasons why the ownership of selected equities should provide significant future gains," he wrote. "While we still firmly believe in this thesis, the continued economic problems experienced throughout the world have rendered our advice incorrect."

∾ DOBSON'S OPTIMISM ∾

Dobson noted that stocks have historically bounced back sharply following a correction, and he suggested, rightly as it turned out, that this would again be the case. To back his argument, he pointed to the sharp drops experienced by big name stocks in the "Great Debacle" of 1929–32 and compared them to the "Super Bear Market" that had begun in 1965. For example, Chrysler fell 96 per cent in the post-1929 period and 83 per cent in the latest bear market. Con Ed dropped 91 per cent after 1929 and 88 per cent in the 1965–74 period. Honeywell fell 90 per cent and 80 per cent, and Westinghouse, 95 per cent and 84 per cent, respectively.

"In the 1929–32 crash, the market was reacting to almost a total wipeout of cumulative corporate earning power," Dobson wrote. "The cards were all on the table, and a depression was taking place as the market was going down. But what of today? We have seen that a great many stocks have already declined as much as they did in the 1930s. Thus, the markdown for a great many stocks has already discounted an economic debacle of the magnitude of the 1930s. Still, unlike 1929–32, the evidence that such a debacle is actually taking place is hardly overwhelming!"

To underscore his optimism in the market, Dobson presented a dramatic table of 30 DJIA stocks from their 1932 lows to 1933 highs. Allied Chemical rose 283 per cent, American Tobacco B 1,250 per cent, Chrysler 1,060 per cent, General Motors 400 per cent, IBM 202 per cent, Procter & Gamble 157 per cent, Union Carbide and Carbon 240 per cent, and Westinghouse Electric 314 per cent. "It must be remembered that these moves came when the United States was still deep in a depression," Dobson noted. "The news background was dismal. These huge advances took place in the blue chip stocks of the period. The moves in many smaller issues were far greater. Typically, half of the total gain in these stocks was achieved in the first few months off the bottom. "If current fears do not become realities," Dobson concluded, "stock market gains from current levels should be large. If these fears are realized, stock prices already appear very close to discounting a similar economic debacle."

Dobson's reassuring prediction of a market recovery seemed highly prescient when in 1975, the Dow Jones Industrial Average jumped by over 38 per cent, followed by a nearly 18 per cent climb in 1976. However, the index dropped by over 17 per cent in 1977. Yet Formula Growth units showed no such pause and were up another 15 per cent in 1977 after increases of 72 per cent and 26 per cent in 1975 and

1976, respectively. But the steep crash in 1973 and 1974 had done its damage, and confidence in Dobson was still low among Formula Growth investors. A $10,000 investment in the units at inception in 1960 were worth $62,425 at the end of 1972 but only $54,709 at the end of 1976. Grumbling grew so intense among certain insiders that a meeting was called at the University Club with the goal of ousting Dobson from Formula Growth. "I heard how unhappy some people were about John's unwillingness to sell, and to see stocks go down and down," says Ian Soutar. "We all loved and respected John, but because he always saw the optimistic side of things, he stayed invested."

Many initial unit holders in Formula Growth Fund were also shareholders in the management company, Formula Growth Limited. Over the years, some of these early investors sold their units and their shares. John Rook left because he thought Dobson and Walter Cottingham were running it too much as a business. Frank Schnabel left because he was more interested in private venture capital. By 1977, the remaining shareholders in the management firm were Lorne Webster, Hugh Hallward, Roger DeSerres, Nassie Godel, Neil Ivory, Drummond Birks, John Dobson, and Peter Mackechnie.

The ownership crisis was sparked when Hugh Hallward announced he was resigning from the board effective 15 June 1977, and asked for his shares to be repurchased. This triggered a battle with other shareholders over what a fair price should be, with Dobson arguing that they had little value since it was his own skills, and those of other Formula Growth employees, that were of value. In fact, Dobson thought it was absurd for more than 80 per cent of the shares in the management firm to be in the hands of people who were not involved in day-to-day investment decisions.

Bob Staples, an auditor for Formula Growth, was engaged as a mediator and evaluated the shares in Formula Growth Ltd. at a book price of $100 each, which in retrospect was well below their true value. Hallward was so angry at the outcome that when he quit in May 1977, he insisted on giving the proceeds of $8,800 from the sale to charity. Among others who also sold were Lorne Webster and Nassie Godel.

In valuing shares in the management company, Dobson compared valuations of other asset management companies, noting many were selling below book value. While shares in Formula Growth may have been worth $200 each in 1972, they were now worth only half, he maintained. "My offer of $90 to each still stands. $100 is if everyone sells so as to relieve me of this problem," Dobson noted in a letter at the time.

In a letter dated 23 June 1977, Dobson vented his frustration and laid all his cards on the table. He argued that only he and Peter Mackechnie should be responsible for the Trust and complained that a "disproportionate amount of time, energy, and goodwill" had been spent on discussing the price of Formula Growth Limited's shares and on ownership. He also noted that there had been a large number of redemptions in the previous six months. He proposed to buy out all shareholders and said that the company should be reorganized so that only directors would attend to the investment side of Formula Growth Fund.

Dobson faced stiff competition for control of Formula Growth from Lorne Webster, who wanted to add it to Bolton Tremblay, an investment management firm that was part of his Prenor Group. He was willing to pay up to $400 a share, four times Dobson's offer. Dobson fought back, accusing Webster of empire building.

"I, Soutar, Taylor and Mackechnie feel that we are entrepreneurs," Dobson told Drummond Birks in a letter written in October 1977. "We invest in and visit owner-run companies and feel that to do our trade requires a climate of owner-management independence and enthusiasm. Clearly, none of us wish to work for Bolton Tremblay or a Lorne Webster-owned company." Dobson also warned that if Bolton Tremblay bought the firm, institutional investors in the Trust fund would be more likely to redeem their units. "I would feel like leaving town if I got [the Trust investors'] support, ran the fund for a couple of years, and then sold it off for a capital profit."

Dobson complained that 82 per cent of the Formula Growth management company was owned by those not directly responsible for making investment decisions. "I am accountable to 300 to 400 of our friends and four pension plans for investment results in a very difficult investment climate. I am frustrated by our inability to get action when the majority agree on what is needed."

In the end, Dobson, with financial support mainly from Drummie Birks, wrote cheques to all the Formula Growth Limited shareholders and took complete control of the management company, which he held on to until the early 1990s. "John paid whatever the units were worth at the time and bought them off the board," says Ian Soutar. "John retained control, which then allowed the firm to exist, quite frankly, because he was able to remain fully invested despite what Peter and others wished."

Soutar notes that, in retrospect, Dobson was on the right side of history. "Looking back over the years, you could see John was always basically right," he says. "It would have been wrong to get rid of all those stocks at that time because they were incredibly cheap. The Fund went up enormously between 1975 and 1983, about 30 per cent a year. So, a lot of people who had hung in ended up making a lot of money. At the time, it was very easy to say that John should have sold out. In retrospect, I think he was right. The good thing about it is that he stayed consistent. He didn't panic." Hugh Hallward was reluctant to discuss the episode. He made efforts to downplay the boardroom tussle, arguing the main issue was leadership. "Walter Cottingham was about to go abroad, and there were questions about whether John would be the best leader," he recalled. "There were many differences of opinion, but it never became personal. I remember Nassie Godel playing a very constructive role."

Godel, who first met Dobson while at business school in 1959 and shared his passion for golf, says one of the conflicts related to the size of Formula Growth. "Some members wanted to bring in more clients and charge more. They wanted a much bigger pot to earn fees on. John was worried that if the Fund got too big, it would be less successful, so he bought the others out."

Peter Mackechnie left Formula Growth in 1977 after Dobson purchased control of the management firm from the dissenting partners. He went on to pursue a short-lived career in the fast-food business by becoming a Long John Silver's franchisee in Western Canada. He later became a successful businessman and stockbroker in Los Angeles and in Vail, Colorado.

Mackechnie today expresses regrets about the failed effort to overthrow Dobson and about the role he played. "I'm not happy with what I did." Dobson never took it personally, however. He felt Mackechnie simply was doing what he felt was right. In fact, Dobson later provided scholarships for Mackechnie's three children to attend university. "When you were a friend of John's, you were always a friend of John's no matter what you did," notes Ian Soutar. "He would give you heck at the time for doing something he didn't like. But then it was over with! One of the great characteristics of the man is that he was loyal to all his friends."

∽ BLACK HATS AND WHITE HATS ∽

Some wounds from the attempted coup never really healed, even though there were efforts to make light of them. At a sixtieth birthday dinner in honour of Dobson held at the Mount Bruno Golf Club in 1988, Peter Mackechnie spoke of the old Formula Growth board meetings, comparing them to an old-style Western movie. "John is waiting in the corral when out of the sunset come the guys in the white hats, the good guys – Roger DeSerres, Donald Johnston, Drummie Birks, Neil Ivory, and Nassie Godel," Mackechnie said. "They are clean shaven, listen to Pat Boone records, and give money to Save the Whales."

"They say hi to Dobson just before some shooting begins up on the hill. The bad guys are approaching. They have on black hats, black shirts covered with dust, scruffy black beards, and their eyes look very mean. They're the bad guys – Hugh Hallward and Lorne Webster. When the shooting dies down and the bad guys have driven off, someone notices over in the trees two men with grey hats on. These are the half-good, half-bad guys. They don't even shave – Walter Cottingham and Peter Mackechnie." The crowd loved it!

CHAPTER 5

Rebirth and Renewal

John let us do what we wanted, but we
had to adhere to the target sheets and focus
on earnings-driven stocks.

— BETTE LOU READE

The late 1970s to the mid-1980s were boom years for Formula Growth. After hitting a low of around $24 in 1974, by 1980, unit values surged fivefold to about $125. By 1987, they had zoomed up to $750, an increase of more than thirty times. From its bear market bottom of 577 on 6 December 1974, the Dow Jones Industrial Average also rebounded strongly but increased "just" fivefold through the 1980s, riding what was known as the "Reagan Bull" to a high of 2,722 on 25 August 1987.

"The boom market lasted until 1987 for us, so you could have done very well," says René Catafago, who started working for Formula Growth as a part-time controller in 1978 and would join full-time a decade later. "One of our clients came in with $100,000 in 1974, and he bought 4,000 units, at the bottom. At the top, those units were worth about $8 million. This was a time of opportunity, because if you had bought in those years, you were almost assured you'd make a lot of money." This was in line with what Dobson had articulated in his 31 December 1974 letter to unit holders.

Before the recovery took off in earnest, and prior to the attempted palace coup, Formula Growth's tiny staff (Dobson, Peter Mackechnie, and Bette Lou Reade) saw the addition of office administrator Barbara Ellis, who remains with the company today. Ellis had been working down the hall from Dobson for a head hunting firm and used to go for lunch with Reade. "Formula Growth hit really bad times in around 1974, and they didn't have a receptionist, so I did a lot of the typing," Ellis recalls. "I got to know them really well, and then Bette Lou offered me the job."

Ellis started in 1977 and was alone on the first day because the three other members of the company happened to be travelling. "It was so small in those days that we'd close the office when they had trips to go visit companies throughout the States," Ellis chuckles. "If it was in Florida or Hilton Head, I was invited, and we all went and had a good time. I remember going to Nashville and visiting companies like Hospital Corp. of America, which went on to become a gigantic hospital management company and a big winner for Formula Growth."

Right from the beginning, Peter Mackechnie and Barbara Ellis would meet at her apartment, and he'd train her about the business, including showing her what Formula Growth called the monthly "break up" or "net asset value" sheets. These allowed them to calculate the monthly valuation of the Fund portfolio. "I wasn't a math wizard, so it was really quite nice that he spent so much time with me," Ellis says. "But I learned it."

Dobson felt that if Ellis was going to work at Formula Growth Fund, she should know what investing was all about, so he helped her buy her first stock. "I can't remember what the company was, but he said I could pay him back when I sold it, if it does well. But if it doesn't do well ... let's just say he was very kind and generous. Luckily, it did do well, and I paid him back and took a trip to Hawaii with the proceeds."

Dobson believed that you had to be an owner to be involved and interested. "So he loaned me money to buy units in Formula Growth Fund, and again I paid him back for that," says Ellis. "He was just great that way. He included me in everything, the meetings and the lunches they had every Tuesday to discuss investments. His main goal, always, was that he wanted it to be fun to work at Formula Growth. And it was. We had a blast!"

Barbara Ellis recalls that occasionally after work, she would go to Bette Lou Reade's house where they would drink martinis and have a laugh. "Bette Lou had a brand-new Mustang, and it was gorgeous. I was so jealous. I told her it was beautiful. She said she got it from Formula Growth because you get a car after five years. I thought, wow! And ten years later, I was still waiting for my car. Thirty-five years later, I'm still waiting for my car. Bette Lou forgot to tell me it was a joke – her mother bought her that car. We still laugh that I never got my 'Formula car.'"

After Peter Mackechnie left Formula Growth, Dobson asked Bette Lou Reade if she would be willing to give up her accounting and bookkeeping duties to concentrate on investments. She reluctantly agreed. "I loved that stuff by then," Reade says. "John wanted me to do stocks, though, because Peter was leaving. I guess that was the beginning of my career." Reade started actively picking stocks. Her father had run his own investment company, so she had been exposed to the business. "It certainly wasn't foreign to me. I had spent enough time around Formula Growth to know what was required and how I had to go about it."

Earlier, Reade had worked in retailing, so it's no surprise that one of her first purchases was fashion firm Liz Claiborne. "John let us do what we wanted, but we had to adhere to the target sheets and focus on earnings-driven stocks," Reade says. "You'd have to go out one and three years. We had these spreadsheet meetings once a week every Tuesday and would order in Laurier BBQ Chicken, and we'd go over the stocks. So, it was really John's criteria that we followed."

Vivacious and attractive, Bette Lou Reade had a knack for talking up executives and extracting every last ounce of information from them. "We'd go to conferences, and Bette Lou would stay at the bar with these guys and get all kinds of very useful information for us," chuckles Ian Soutar. "Sometimes she'd come back and tell John that particular investments could be in deep trouble for such and such reasons, because 'so and so would say ... ' John would sometimes ignore completely what she had said. In some cases she was right, and John was wrong, certainly in the short term. Bette Lou was our important hidden treasure in terms of getting us information about stuff that John would have never been able to get hold of."

"Dobson would often sic Bette Lou on some company," remembers long-time Fund manager Ted Ashford. "In her own way, she would learn a lot. She asked the best questions. She smelled a rat with Comp-U-Card, and the CEO is now in prison. She didn't like his eyes, his answers, or the smell."

Reade recalls buying a company for the Fund in the mid-1980s. The company, headed by Barry Minkow, was called ZZZZ BEST, and it was supposedly in the business of carpet cleaning and insurance restoration. "The IPO was presented to me by a firm out West, and I met Minkow over lunch. His manners were absolutely incredibly awful," Reade says. "He was twenty years old, and he commenced to tell us that he had gone to military school. So I thought, hmm, no one that's been to military school comes out with manners like that. So I was suspicious. Anyway, I bought the stock and it went straight up. I think it doubled. That was enough for me. I sold the whole thing. A year later, Minkow was in jail. The thing was a total fraud. And John said to me, "Just think, it could have been ZZZZ WORST!"

∞ THE NETWORK ∞

Critical to the investment strategy of Dobson and his team was travelling across the continent to visit with the people running the businesses in which Formula Growth invested. The intent was to gain the first-hand knowledge he thought was essential. Dobson also built a network of regional brokerages, fund managers, and contacts in the United States that was second to none. This generated ideas as well as tips on growth companies that were poised for success.

"We held day-long conferences in places like Newport, Rhode Island, and Hilton Head, South Carolina, to develop this network of people we had around the country," says Bette Lou Reade. "They'd be attended by stockbrokers and money managers who contributed meaningfully to the success of the Fund. A key to our success was getting to know really smart people throughout the United States, from big cities and small cities, who were doing the same kind of things. They'd share their ideas with us and became good friends. These turned out to be pre-eminent managers, so it was a collection of very smart individuals who became extraordinarily successful."

ALEX HAMMOND-CHAMBERS

One of the earliest members of this network was Alex Hammond-Chambers, a prominent UK money manager and investor who would later become chairman of the Scottish firm Ivory & Sime. He had just joined the firm when he first met Dobson in the summer of 1966, having previously worked with Formula Growth director Neil Ivory at a company that was a predecessor of Pembroke Management. (Ivory, the grandson of the founder of Ivory & Sime, went on to co-found Pembroke Management with Scott Taylor, Ian Soutar, and Clifford Larock. He was also the brother-in-law of Scott Fraser, who co-founded Jarislowsky Fraser with Canadian money guru Stephen Jarislowsky.)

"Dobson and Ian Soutar hunted in pairs or teams when looking for and visiting small growth companies," says Hammond-Chambers. "Since I was also managing American money, I joined them." The trio had the same investment approach. They were looking for good, well-managed, smaller growth companies in which the management had a significant financial stake. They spent a lot of time on price potential or target sheets, looking at what the companies would make over three to five years, instead of a matter of months. "We'd do our research and determine what growth rates and terminal price-earnings ratios to expect," explains Hammond-Chambers. "Then we'd decide if there was a good return to be made on it." In contrast, today's market is dominated by value investors who look at what is the price potential given the earnings forecast for the quarter and the current price-earnings ratio. "No one today looks very far forward when investing," he adds. "In fact, many stock market participants seem to just day trade."

What impressed Alex Hammond-Chambers was Dobson's incredible discipline. If the price potentials looked cheap on a long-term basis, he would top up the holding. But if it looked expensive, he'd cut it. "If it was a good company, he was happy to own a little bit of it on the grounds that he'd want to go back into it one day when the price was more attractive. If you sell a holding, you're inclined to give up watching it, which he didn't want to do," Hammond-Chambers notes. "Dobson typically had quite long lists of sixty to eighty stocks. He'd have two parts in a portfolio: one for major investments and another for his 'nursery' portfolio, in which he'd put in a small amount into the stock and watch it grow."

Hammond-Chambers and Dobson would attend conferences together, share ideas, and price potentials, and then play a little golf. "We weren't competing. Dobson had a great network, and we did, too. We exploited the opportunities of going around to regional brokerages and finding local companies. Regional brokers knew who the good people and the good companies were."

Ivory & Sime and Formula Growth rang up some big winners between the mid-1970s and the mid-1980s in what Alex Hammond-Chambers described as the "golden era." Most of these gains were in technology and specialty retailing, such as fast food. Stellar performers included Shared Medical Systems Inc., a health-related computer services firm; orange-juice giant Tropicana; big-box retailer Toys R Us; and the high-end tool supplier, Snap-on Tools. Dobson was patient and focused on the right things, Hammond-Chambers notes. "That's one of the reasons he was so successful. Today, things are more complicated. People look at things that are not as relevant. That may be good for egos, but not for the money they manage."

STEVE RIVEN

Steve Riven was one of the early sell-side regional brokers who worked with Formula Growth. Today a senior managing partner at Avondale Partners in Nashville, he got into the securities business in 1966 and credits Dobson with his success. "John was the most helpful guy I've ever seen. If it hadn't been for him, I wouldn't have been successful. I've been in business for forty-seven years thanks to him and Ian Soutar."

Riven's parents hailed from Montreal, and he had a first cousin who went to McGill with Soutar. "I was living in Nashville," Riven recalls, "and had registered to enter the securities business in 1965 with J.C. Bradford" (a famous brokerage house). "My cousin encouraged me to go to Montreal and meet this one guy: Ian Soutar." Riven and Soutar got together and discussed companies and stocks they were following. It was then that Soutar introduced Riven to Dobson.

Dobson took over the networking from there. "He was like a tiger," says Riven. "He knew everybody and introduced me to them. He could get you in the front door, and then the first guy you met would introduce you to another, and it would snowball from there. He was the best networker, and everyone loved him."

Riven sold research and equities to Formula Growth for twenty years while at J.C. Bradford & Co., including such winners as Hospital Corp. of America and Blue Bell Jeans. Riven continued to do business with Formula Growth when he moved to Equitable Securities and later set up Avondale, an investment banking and wealth management firm. "When I founded Avondale in 2001, John called and said he wanted to be the first trade through our firm. And he was."

Dobson's approach, Steve Riven notes, was simple but consistent: buy good people and good companies for the long term. "He believed in people. He took some risks as well, based on people running companies. But he got to know them, and if he was confident in them, he'd support them. To me, John Dobson is a legend. He helped many kids go to college and never looked for any recognition."

SCOTT TAYLOR

Scott Taylor is a long-standing partner of Ian Soutar's at Pembroke Management, which manages the highly successful GBC family of mutual funds. Founded in 1968, Pembroke's investment philosophy was similar to that of Formula Growth's. While more focused on

Canada, it also invested in US stocks. Taylor and Soutar used to meet with Dobson and his team at least once a week to discuss stocks and world events. "John was the kind of guy you could take to readily, because he was so friendly," says Taylor. "He had strong convictions of what was good or not good. I've always admired his integrity and networking skills. He was a great believer in getting out and talking to people." For many years, Pembroke acted as a consultant to Formula Growth, providing a second opinion on companies. "It's nice to run things by someone," explains Taylor. "We were familiar with the names involved with Formula Growth. We were like a partner, and got the benefit of hearing what John Dobson and Peter Mackechnie thought. Dobson was very generous, and he thought there were advantages in looking at the market together."

The two companies even invested together in a lot of names and had similar investment criteria. The only rivalry between Pembroke and Formula Growth was around Christmas time when they had bet on stocks for the next year in a friendly, informal competition, a tradition similar to the Dobson Dinners.

TED ASHFORD

Professional investor Ted Ashford had also known Dobson for decades and bonded over a mutual interest in investing. "We started turning up at the same places, and we got to know each other," Ashford says. "I was always interested because John and Ian [Soutar] would appraise companies for their upside potential in a very disciplined fashion. They weeded out companies that didn't have potential, causing you to focus on the ones that did."

Ashford and Dobson would attend the same regional investment meetings in Atlanta and elsewhere, and once the meetings were done, they'd all play golf for a couple of days in what Dobson called a "balanced program." Ashford managed a growth-stock fund and then set up his own firm, which managed small-cap growth stocks. "We weren't really competitors with Formula Growth since they were in Canada and we were in the United States," he says. "Like them, we wanted to get excellent investment results, and didn't want to be big." Ashford began calculating a company's potential the same way as Dobson and Ian Soutar did. "This way, we could speak the same language. When you have three different guys looking at a management, you come up with different questions." The trio would often call on private companies and look for opportunities together, mainly on the US west coast.

Ted Ashford and Dobson stayed friends for many years and went on golf cruises together to the Mediterranean, New Zealand, the Baltic, and along the Rhine River. "We'd be on a boat, then golf for the day, and get back on the boat. We'd talk investments on these trips, but it wasn't a purposeful investment trip." They both also had a mutual interest in entrepreneurship. "US investments were John's specialty, but he wanted Canada to have the same kind of entrepreneurship, and he'd work hard on this."

JOHN LOWENBERG

John Lowenberg, who runs an investment partnership called Anvil Management Co., met Dobson and Ian Soutar while working as an institutional salesman at Robinson Humphrey in Atlanta. He was introduced by colleague Bobby London, whom Dobson liked to refer to as "Big Bad Bobby" – he was 5'4". London was a charming man and a nifty dresser who often wore white shoes and a cashmere topcoat and who knew Dobson and Soutar from frequent trips to Canada. "John was an instant charmer," says Lowenberg. "It turned out that we knew many of the same friends from Scotland, such as Alex Hammond-Chambers, and shared a mutual love for growth companies."

Dobson and Soutar would always sit in the front row at Robinson Humphrey's investment seminars and ask good, perceptive questions, says Lowenberg. "We would go visit companies together, because I had an analytical and business background." They also held meetings with companies and clients in such places as Sea Island, Georgia, playing golf or tennis during the day, while the CEOs would talk about their companies in the evenings.

Lowenberg says some lucrative investments in the southeast United States resulted from this close business relationship, including Cousins Properties, a huge Atlanta-based real estate developer that reaped more than 20 per cent annual returns over thirty years. Formula Growth got in early with retailer Dollar General, when it had fewer than 100 stores compared to about 5,000 today, and Theragenics, which produced a novel treatment for prostate cancer; its stock jumped from $2 to $60 between 1988 and 1992. Other winners included Scientific Atlanta, Office Depot, Humana, Charter Medical, and Genuine Parts.

Coca-Cola Company, while based in Atlanta, was given a pass. "It wasn't growing quick enough. It was growing only 12 per cent," quips Lowenberg. "John Dobson had a tremendous nose for business," he adds. "He was open to any venture and loved getting to know the company chairman, relaxing and chatting. He knew I had my own formulas, and we'd key them together and come up with the best companies that fit Pembroke and Formula Growth. We were looking at 17 to 20 per cent returns, for fast-growing companies." Lowenberg contends that Dobson's nose for business was at least as good as that of legendary investor Peter Lynch: "He was always jovial but an extremely hard worker, putting in fourteen-hour days."

BOBBY LONDON

Bobby London was only about twenty-five years old when he met Dobson while working with Robinson Humphrey. "I worked with John Lowenberg but started calling on Dobson shortly after being hired. I was an institutional broker, but since all major accounts in the US were covered and no one was covering Canada, I decided to go there. So I showed up in Montreal in the early 1970s on a day when there were still eight inches of snow on the ground. I rushed to my first meeting with John, Peter [Mackechnie], and Bette Lou [Reade], and they all laughed when I walked in. I was wearing a light blue suit and white shoes, without a coat."

Bobby London and Dobson became close friends, and they'd visit companies together in the Atlanta area. London also attended the Dobson Dinner in San Francisco for about eight years after moving to Montgomery Securities in San Francisco. "John was so generous, probably the most enjoyable of all my clients," says London. "He took me under his wing and introduced me to everyone. He wasn't a tough guy, just a pleasure and a gentleman. He had a great sense of humour and was gracious even about bad news."

ROBERT POWER

Robert Power, an international equity salesman at Hambrecht & Quist – a well-known New York-based technology, venture capital, and underwriting company in the early 1980s – was also impressed by the warm reception he received by the Formula Growth team. "One of the things to understand about Formula Growth is that unlike virtually anybody else, they believed in being nice to people rather than having this adversarial relationship," Power notes. "I was made to feel welcome from the get-go."

Power found Dobson to be no less than remarkable, able to cut to the heart of things. "I always admired how quick and decisive he was. He would know instantly if something would appeal to him, and he was very loyal to those he dealt with. Formula Growth has probably got the greatest long-term record of any investment entity that I'm aware of, because their network was composed of people who were like them."

Hambrecht & Quist had many tech underwritings in which Formula Growth was interested, and Power used to visit Montreal fifteen to twenty times a year, and sometimes more. Power says he introduced Formula Growth in the late 1990s to what would become one of its biggest winners: Celgene Corp., a biotech company. Another company that did very well was First Financial Management Corp. "Formula Growth wanted growth. They didn't care from where, but it had to be growth. So they were very focused on technology and health care."

Power says one of the Formula Growth team's strongest features was the fact that they had good instincts. "They knew a good story when they heard one, and this distinguished them from other people. Their experience and network would have played a bigger part in their decision-making process than it would in other organizations. If they blamed us for any failures, I never knew about it. Formula Growth has lived through ups and downs of growth stocks, and you need strong stomachs for that. I never remember them blaming us for any disasters."

DICK LILLY

Dick Lilly, a former analyst for Raymond James and JW Charles, also had extensive dealings with Dobson from the mid-1970s to the early 1990s and was impressed by his uncanny ability to read research and pick out ideas to invest in. "I was focused on smaller emerging companies then, and brought some ideas to John. I thought he was one of the smartest money managers I ever came across."

Along with John Templeton, Dobson caught electronics retailer Circuit City at an early stage of development in the 1970s and early 1980s, a time when it was called Wards, and had a spectacular run with it. He sold before the company fizzled and ultimately went bankrupt. For a while, Circuit City was Formula Growth's largest single holding and was ranked the best stock on the NYSE in the 1990s. "He was one of the first to recognize the opportunities presented by big-box stores," says Dick Lilly. "Other big-box retailers that became home runs for the Fund were Price Club and Home Depot."

Dobson was a master at managing risk and reward. His track record showed consistent returns, notes Lilly. He believed in the quality of management and took a hands-on interest in what he was investing in. "He used to visit many companies a day, 200 plus a year," says Lilly, who headed up the research department at Raymond James between 1974 and 1987. "He was constantly travelling, visiting companies throughout North America, maintaining good relationships."

Dobson had an extraordinary ability for identifying small, emerging growth companies before they became big names – and finding the right talent to help him get the job done. Decade after decade, this proved to be his investment hallmark.

CHAPTER 6

New Blood

I always felt John Dobson and I were like
"two ships destined to meet."

— RANDY KELLY

Bob Staples first met John Dobson in 1974 through Formula Growth's auditor, Russ Bremner. "John was a character. Very bright, very much in the know, very connected with current events," recalls Staples, who worked for Gardner McDonald (later acquired by Touche Ross, and now Deloitte Touche). Staples would soon become audit partner for Formula Growth, keeping that role for close to thirty years until his retirement in 2003. "The Fund was very small in the 1970s, especially after the market crash, and they all worked in a tiny office. But I witnessed tremendous growth over the years."

While Dobson always introduced Staples as his auditor, Staples also acted as a business adviser and family counsellor. "It's a twenty-four-hour job in a small practice like that," Staples notes. "I was the outside source for a lot of people to bounce ideas off. I also helped them deal with many personal issues: breakups, divorces, you name it. It was not just a business relationship, but a friendship."

Staples became known as "The Captain" because he took Dobson and members of his network out on his sailboat. Then, one day, he told Dobson about a young auditor working for him at Touche Ross, named Randy Kelly. It would prove to be a fateful introduction. "Randy and I worked on some big accounts together, and we had a lot of respect for each other," Staples recalls. "So I got Randy to do the audit at Formula Growth, and I suggested to Dobson that if he needed a young guy, to talk to Randy."

∽ RANDY KELLY ∾

Kelly couldn't have come from a more different background than Dobson. Growing up in the working-class Montreal neighbourhood of LaSalle, he attended Verdun High School like his father. "My background is very blue collar," Kelly says proudly. "My father drove a train. He dropped out of school in grade 9 to help his family in the late 1930s during the Great Depression. My mother was born in Sherbrooke. She too had to drop out in grade 8 or 9. I grew up with parents who had great principles, great morals, and great ethics – but little education. So the dominant thing was to get an education. 'You have to get an education, Randy.' That's all I ever remember my parents saying."

Kelly describes his father as "one of the brightest people I know." He also had a passion for cards and, without knowing it, a deep understanding of probabilities, skills that would serve his son well for a career in the stock market. "Through my dad and my upbringing, I remember always being interested in mathematics and probabilities. And I remember my father teaching me how to play Monopoly, and poker, and every other card game when I was a little kid."

Kelly used to go to Montreal's Blue Bonnets racetrack with his father, where he initially made a little money and then lost. "I quickly recognized that the math behind racetrack returns had a hole in it, because the track has to take 20 per cent to make money. So, in the long haul, the bettor won't make money. A racetrack or a casino is not a closed loop. There is always a 'rake' for the house, so players can't do well. When I explained that to my father, he said, 'I just like to watch the horses go.' In other words, it was fun for him. But that wasn't enough for me."

After graduating from Verdun High School in 1973, Kelly took the proceeds from his summer job as a busboy at the LaSalle Legion Hall and started to invest in the stock market. He considered it the ultimate card game. Unlike the racetrack with its rake, a card game is a closed loop. No money leaks out. It remains in the loop and accrues to the winner, Kelly explains. "If you actually do your work, the stock market is like being at a card table. In fact, it is a card table where the 'house' pours in more money via the growth of the under-lying companies and growth in GDP – so even better! If you stay and make the right moves, watch the cards being dealt, and have steady nerves, you will win over the long term. But don't fall asleep."

Kelly recalls those days as being a good time to buy because stock prices were really low, so he started buying stocks and mak-ing money." Coincidentally, this was at the same time Dobson was imploring his customers to stay the course in 1974. "As a young guy, probably around eighteen, I think I spent my money quite quickly and had fun."

That summer, Kelly went to work at Northern Electric (the prede-cessor to Nortel), expediting goods between the office and the plant in Montreal's Pointe-Saint-Charles district. "I liked what I was doing at Northern and decided to switch to commerce from science. I went back to Dawson College" (a junior college, or CEGEP, in Montreal) "and finished the required two-year program. I got accepted at Concordia University, but not the more highbrow McGill that was so near and dear to John Dobson, because my grades were just okay."

While studying commerce at Concordia, Kelly lived at home with his mother, who had separated from his father. "I had to keep mak-ing money, to chip in to help support my mother. I remember when my parents started to break up, they'd argue about money, and I con-cluded that it could solve a lot of problems. I think a little differently today, that money can't solve problems, but it sure doesn't hurt. But back then, I always wanted to make money since I thought I could help out the family if I had it. So between liking money, liking math, and liking games of chance, I fell in love with stocks. I also really loved to work. I've liked every job I've ever had. I find it keeps me out of trouble. The stock market is perfect for me – it's very challenging and keeps me busy."

After graduating from Concordia, Kelly decided to go into accounting because it seemed practical. "When I went to the job recruiting room in Concordia, there was a big board filled with job offerings from all the Big Eight (now the Big Four) CA firms, so I applied for two or three of those and got interviews with all of them. I had what they wanted: a B.Com with honours in accounting." He had secondary interviews over lunch with a few partners, and Touche Ross (now Deloitte Touche) seemed to be the best. So he signed on in August 1978.

Kelly studied for his chartered accounting (CA) degree at McGill by taking night courses for two years and obtained his designation at the age of twenty-four. "I had a blast at Touche Ross because there was a constant stream of young people coming in. I would get good clients, which was helpful for my growth, because I would do audits for public companies such as United Westburne, Bank of Montreal, etc. I met high-level executives and learned how to talk to them, which helped me later in the investment business."

Randy Kelly had a knack for speaking and relating to people and moved up the ranks quite quickly. He was working hard as an accountant and was busy teaching and lecturing in the CA programs at McGill and Concordia. "At around age twenty-five, I wanted to become a partner, and I thought it was a great career path," he says. "You can become anything once you're a CA, even more so today, with the world being over-regulated."

Bob Staples was one of Kelly's bosses at Touche and asked him to audit a client, Formula Growth. Kelly was reluctant. "I didn't want to because I'd never heard of it, and it seemed kind of small," he recalls. "He said it ran two high-profile mutual funds whose clients included high net-worth people and big institutions like the Royal Bank."

Kelly says today that he always felt John Dobson and he were like "two ships destined to meet." But that wasn't how it looked at first. He came in as the auditor and met Dobson, Bette Lou Reade, and Barbara Ellis. René Catafago was also working as an external accountant at that time, performing all the internal accounting for Formula Growth's funds. "He becomes my go-to guy during an audit. I come in and I'm fascinated by the place and I see a list of stocks that I've never heard of, all of them American, small and mid-capped stocks, and they're growing like crazy."

Kelly's first impression of John was not all that favourable, however. "I thought he was crazy," he admits. "That remained my impression for a few years, even when I worked with him. Over time, I understood him better. He was the most intellectually honest person I've ever seen. And he was so focused, passionate, and energetic, with an unbounded curiosity."

Kelly did two or three annual audits, requiring him to be in the Formula Growth office for a week or so per year. He got to know the company's tiny staff. "John barked at me for looking at the petty cash, worrying about that. It was immaterial. I got to know his idiosyncrasies and thought he was fascinating, and he clearly was a success. I could see from the portfolio that a lot of the stocks he had invested in had skyrocketed. In 1981–82, when technology was exploding, the Fund was on fire. Things were spectacular. I was mesmerized."

While auditing Formula Growth, Kelly says he recognized the enormous leverage potential in the investment business. "I compared it with the accounting profession and charging myself out at an hourly rate and hoping to become a partner. I started to see the challenge of finding these great stocks and wanted to be part of it."

In the fall of 1983, when Kelly came in to do a half-day systems audit with René Catafago, Dobson announced that he wanted to hire somebody young. Kelly suggested a colleague of his at Touche Ross, but Dobson shot back, "I want you." Kelly, still aiming to be a partner at Touche Ross, told Dobson that at twenty-seven, he wasn't young anymore. "I was working in a highbrow accounting firm and told him I'd get him a younger guy."

Dobson was relentless and took Kelly to a few investment meetings in Montreal so he could see how he operated. "I thought it was cool. I had a long lunch with Bob Staples, and he told me I'd be out of my mind to not take this opportunity with John. So I did. I got on board in early 1984 as treasurer."

Kelly's modest origins were not a hindrance. On the contrary. Drummond Birks, Dobson's old friend, was enthusiastic about the idea of hiring Kelly. "If you want somebody to succeed you, they should be from Verdun," Birks advised. "That was near and dear to John," says Kelly, "to have a guy from the other side of the tracks. Maybe he saw it in his father, Sydney, because he came from a more pedestrian background."

But soon after starting, Kelly decided Formula Growth wasn't for him. "After three months, I wasn't getting close enough to the stocks, and the accounting was getting dull because there wasn't enough to do. So I told John I was getting bored and wanted out. John and I had this catastrophic argument. It got really nasty, and I thought that he'll either fire me, or I'll quit. So, I'm basically done."

Dobson called the next day, and the two reconciled. "I told him things had to change, that I had to give the accounting back to René Catafago, the external accountant, and visit companies. I wanted more input on the portfolio," Kelly says. "I told him I'll supervise the accounting and treasury, but I'll delegate it outside. At that point, I got more involved with John on the portfolio and got in on the calls and on the road. I learned about the business and applied the knowledge I had as a CA, analyzing financial results. Later on, I became a chartered financial analyst, so I could progress even further."

When Kelly signed on in 1984, Formula Growth Fund had about $36 million US in assets under management, and the institutional fund, Formula Unit Trust, had about $55 million (US). There were 133,000 units, and the price was $270 (US)/$347 (CAN) per unit (compared with $5,200 (US)/$5,400 (CAN) in mid-2013).

"Unfortunately, when I came on board, it was a tough period for Formula Growth because 1983 was the crescendo of a tech boom," recalls Kelly. "The tech stocks were hot in the early 1980s, and the unit price topped out at $500 in mid-1983. By the time I bought my first units, they were $300 each. John loaned me the money to buy my first thirty or so units. My first units alone today would be worth over $140,000. He loaned me $10,000, which has long been paid off."

∽ BLACK MONDAY ∾

Then came the stock market crash of 19 October 1987. In what has become known as Black Monday, the Dow Jones Industrial Average fell by 508 points, or 22.6 per cent, from 2,246.73 to 1,738.74, its biggest one-day percentage decline ever. The crash began in Hong Kong and spread west to Europe, hitting the United States after other markets had already declined by a significant margin.

The crash has since been largely blamed on automated computer trading that forced sell orders when the market turned down, exacerbated by negative market psychology. Following the stock market crash, a group of thirty-three leading economists from around the world met in December in Washington, DC, and collectively predicted that "the next few years could be the most troubled since the 1930s." Nevertheless, the DJIA was positive for the 1987 calendar year. It opened on 2 January 1987 at 1,897 points and closed on 31 December 1987 at 1,939 points. However, the average did not regain its 25 August 1987 closing high of 2,722 points until almost two years later.

Formula Growth units lost nearly 34 per cent of their value in October 1987 and ended the year down 7 per cent. Just before the crash, the Formula Growth team was having its weekly meeting, enjoying Laurier BBQ chicken in the office, when Dobson received a phone call. Unknown to the rest, it was from legendary investor Sir John Templeton. "John gets mad that our chicken lunch gets interrupted, and I hear him yelling 'no!' gruffly into the phone multiple times, and he hangs up," remembers Kelly. "I ask who it was, and he says, 'Sir John.' It turned out he wanted to come into the Fund as a customer, and I told Barbara [Ellis] to phone him back and tell him we'd find a way to get him invested from his offshore base. I leave the chicken lunch to talk to Templeton's people. Templeton invests in August of 1987, putting $5 million into Formula Growth Fund."

René Catafago remembers the episode, although slightly differently. "In 1987, just before the crash, John Templeton called and spoke with Dobson and said, 'I'd like to invest in your Fund.' Now Templeton is the god of investments, and they were friends before that. But Dobson tells him, 'No, I don't take new money, I don't want your money.' And he just hung up on him! So he tells Bette Lou [Reade] and Randy [Kelly], and they thought he was out of his mind! They say, 'Do you realize how important it would be to have Templeton investing his own money in your Fund? Call him back!' So he calls him back and says, 'Yeah, yeah I spoke with Randy and Bette Lou, and we should take your money.' So, sure enough, Templeton puts money in, invests in August of 1987. By October, there is a crash, and a couple months later, Templeton had lost 40 per cent of his money." (He astutely doubled down his position after the crash, trying to recoup his losses by buying twice as much.) "So timing, if you get the entry point right, can be everything! With the years, he made it all back, and at some point, around 2000, Templeton was the largest single unit holder of Formula Growth. He had around $40 million with us, either himself or through his foundations. And he stayed very, very loyal to the Fund until a few years before he passed away, when he had to redo his estate."

Templeton invested in Formula Growth because he believed that it had the right investment approach, and he trusted Dobson implicitly. "I remember when we reached a certain amount, he congratulated us on the milestone," recalls René Catafago. "I think when we reached $900 a unit, he said it's a milestone of 100 times our money. After that, the unit went from $900 to $5,400 in Canadian dollars, which is another six times! So, at some point, we were a printing machine, and we only charged 1 per cent on the funds under investment, which was much less than anyone else in the business. Everybody realized it and wanted to give us money."

⚭ NEW TROOPS ⚭

After more than a decade of doing the books externally or part-time, René Catafago was brought into Formula Growth as a full-time employee in 1987. Catafago had known about Formula Growth since the late 1960s because his brother, Philip, had been the company's auditor in those days. "I remember him telling me that there was a beautiful fund, and people were making a lot of money with it. He said it was Formula Growth, but he couldn't invest in it because he was the auditor of the company."

In 1972, while studying for his CA, Catafago went to work for auditor Russ Bremner, who happened to have trained Philip as a CA as well. In 1976, Catafago installed new accounting systems for differentiating between US and Canadian dollars at Formula Growth. The Fund was still tiny and was staffed by only Dobson, Bette Lou Reade, and Peter Mackechnie.

"The first time I meet Dobson, he comes in and they tell him there's this bright auditor asking too many questions. He gives me shit. He says he doesn't have time for number crunchers. He can't waste time giving me useless information." Catafago says he went back to Bremner's partner, Bob Staples, and told him, "'I'm not working at this place ever again. Don't ever send me there.' Just to make a long story short, I'm still here. That's about thirty-five years later."

Dobson was always against administration and red tape, says Catafago. "He was Mr Entrepreneur. He loved to buy stocks, sell stocks, and he wanted to create profits for unit holders. He never had time for anything to do with administrative work. He was not into it. It wasn't his forte."

While Catafago may have failed to convince Dobson what good things the back office can do, the two became good friends. "When I met him, after the initial fight, he asked my name, and I said René Catafago. 'Too complicated,' he said. 'I'll call you The Cat.' After that, my office started calling me The Cat. Later on, all my friends started calling me The Cat. And I'm now The Cat to everybody."

∞ GROUP THERAPY ∞

Dobson liked to get people together in a group because he believed in the power of teamwork. He once invited investors in the Formula Unit Trust fund for a sailboat expedition on the St Lawrence as a "bonding" experience. The participants ended up getting a lot more than they bargained for. As Peter Mackechnie recalls, "Bob Staples (the Captain), brought his sailboat to a dock on the St Lawrence River, and about a dozen members of the Formula Unit Trust fund were invited on board. During the expedition, there was this terrible crash, and we couldn't figure out what the hell had happened. It turns out the boat had run aground, and its masthead shattered. Bob comes from the end of the boat with a cut that had opened up on his head. I had a smaller cut, but still needed stitches. People were lying around dazed. Bob Thompson from the Royal Bank was the most seriously injured and was taken to the Montreal General Hospital. He got twenty-one stitches in his forehead. He came back and insisted on getting back on the boat. The moral of this was that Dobson felt that having all the customers together with Bette Lou Reade and me and some other Formula Growth friends was just good for business. That was one day, though, when it was not too good."

Two months after René Catafago formally joined Formula Growth, the stock market crashed. He lost much of his savings and feared Formula Growth might go bankrupt because it was going downhill so quickly. "For three years, from 1987 to 1990, the markets tried to rally. The unit value went from $750 to about $380. And some customers were really mad at us, asking what we were doing, yelling at us for losing their money, and we said we haven't changed. We invest for the long term."

Catafago rose to become CFO and then executive vice-president and an owner of the firm, but he never played an active role in picking stocks. "Dobson had this idea that you either pick stocks, or you're in charge of administration. He said to me once, 'Your forte is administration and not stocks, so concentrate, because trying to do both is not a good idea.'"

Just a few months after the October 1987 crash, another key player joined Formula Growth. Kim Holden, Bette Lou Reade's daughter, came in to replace Barbara Ellis while she was on maternity leave. One of Holden's major selling points was that she could actually handle a computer in an office where there were none. Everything at Formula Growth was being done manually. "We read the *Wall Street Journal* every weekend, and we kept the prices," recalls Reade. "We'd take the quotes right out of the newspaper. We were very basic." (Formula Growth Fund valuations were calculated twice a month for purchases and redemptions.)

In that environment, Holden looked like Microsoft founder Bill Gates (his company had just gone public in 1986). "All I had to do was buy a computer and install some basic software packages, and they thought I was genius," she recalls with a smile. "So they asked me to stay after my six-month stint." Holden had just graduated with a degree in economics from Carleton University in Ottawa. "I had skipped a couple years of education and graduated at twenty, so I was a little young to know what I wanted to do. This opportunity presented itself, and I had grown up with investments all around me. So I decided to take the job and learn a little bit about the business."

Soon after being hired full-time, Randy Kelly suggested that Holden do the CFA exams and learn the business. Even though she hadn't had any previous accounting or business experience, she sailed through three years of the financial analyst's course, obtaining her CFA in 1990. Dobson immediately encouraged her to put some money to work. "One of John's great strengths was his willingness to teach other people. And one unusual thing about him was that he taught by allowing people to take risks," she says. "So many other people would be worried about the downside in allowing someone very new to take such a risk. They'd tell me to do my research, think of three ideas, and then they'd go over it. John would just tell me to go buy some stocks."

Holden could not have started at a better time. "After a very rough start to the decade, the early 1990s were absolutely stupendous years," she enthuses. "I think from 1991, the Fund went up sharply every year, for five years. They were just fantastic, and the US dollar was at its peak against the Canadian dollar. The performance was achieved without hedging or derivatives, just a plain vanilla, long-term horizon. The entire decade turned out to be a strong one for us."

Formula Growth's stellar performance during the 1990s (the unit price jumped over nine times, from $380 to $3,600 US) was due partly to these favourable market conditions. But a much bigger factor was Dobson's discipline, along with his fearless investment approach. It was not something for the faint of heart.

CHAPTER 7

The Growth Formula

Those things that are often perceived as
risky have the most opportunity.

— IAN SOUTAR

Throughout its history, Formula Growth has not hesitated to invest in unconventional companies, the type that may not pass muster in a traditional blue-chip portfolio of established names. While it has almost always played with publicly listed stocks, many are at such an early stage of development that investing in them could best be described as engaging in a kind of public-venture capital. Too small or too unproven, these companies are clearly not ready for so-called prime time investing by mainstream investors.

This approach has been an essential part of Formula Growth's game plan from its earliest days, with generally terrific results. Occasionally, however, some big catches have got away. Back in 1970, for example, when an upstart retailer from Arkansas decided to go public with his growing chain of discount department stores that concentrated on small, neglected markets, John Dobson decided to check it out.

"When the great companies were becoming public, we had a look at them and tried to get in really early," he later explained. "We had an opportunity to invest in Wal-Mart right at the beginning. I even had dinner with Sam Walton. But we never bought Wal-Mart. We thought it was too expensive." It was a rare misstep in a remarkable career.

"Fortunately, we did buy Home Depot very early on, before the big-box formula really took off," Dobson continued. "Ian Soutar and

I went to visit the first store they opened up in Atlanta. So we were doing things that were really unconventional, and to make really big money, that's what you need to do."

The idea was to get in on innovative ventures, to look for a business plan that is brand new and perhaps not well understood, and where the people involved may be inexperienced or at times not even regarded as the best. Ideally, their ventures turn out to be huge successes. The founders' lack of experience, or the challenge they faced in explaining their product, could even be assets in Dobson's eyes. "When the companies all are well recognized and everyone understands the story, they become well priced in the market, so you don't make the kind of returns that Formula Growth is looking for," Dobson explained.

Because of this approach, there have been failures as well. "But the successes are so early in their life cycles that they tend to overshadow the failures," Dobson said. "The failure rate may be much higher, but the success rate is so big and so powerful that it overshadows it."

This investment approach has meant that Formula Growth has focused mainly on technology, pharmaceuticals, speciality retailing, restaurants, financials, and some small industrial companies. It has generally shied away from commodities, with the exception of oil, because these companies tend to be cyclical and hard to judge. If Formula Growth owned a cyclical, it tried to come in very early, when the growth was the fastest off the bottom.

But Formula Growth also recognizes how difficult it is to judge where the bottom is and generally keeps away from this space. As for utilities, they were and still are too dull to consider. And while Formula Growth is always looking for the next "big idea," it also looks for "real" companies. It avoids investing in concept stocks and keeps away from those reliant on a fad with outsized future expectations. "A fad by nature is just that – a fad," said Dobson. "It comes quickly and leaves just as fast. Where is Pokémon now?" During the dot-com bubble of the late 1990s, the market was filled with "weekend" investors chasing such fads. "People were no longer investing. They were speculating."

Such speculation was one of the reasons for the 1929 stock market crash, Dobson noted. Rumours, innuendo, and an army of day traders caused markets to swing schizophrenically from day to day. The aftermath of this was a terrible bear market hangover that left the investment community trying for years to pick up the pieces and rebuild.

Financials have also been a big part of the Formula Growth portfolio, but usually not traditional banks. Rather, the Fund was always interested in a financial company with a new idea. One example was Jackson National Insurance, a firm that provided specialized insurance products and annuities. The spectacular gains earned by Formula Growth when the company was bought out by British insurer Prudential PLC provided the initial funding for the John Dobson Foundation.

∽ "WHAT ARE YOU DOING?" ∾

"Formula Growth was typically unconventional," says Ian Soutar. "Most people would not understand some of its choices at all. They'd look at it and ask 'What are you doing?'"

Dobson said the goal was to find solid individual companies and have the patience to wait for them to succeed rather than relying on traditional tools of market timing or economic factors. Formula Growth has always taken a bottom-up approach, looking at individual companies rather than starting with an industry or macro approach. "I long ago concluded that the best results are obtained over a longer time period by investing in successful companies that are making above-average returns on shareholders' equity, that have rapidly increasing earnings, and that are selling at historically low prices. I knew going in that we would experience setbacks, which we probably wouldn't be able to identify in advance. But the rewards have always justified the risks."

René Catafago says that Dobson had a simple formula for picking stocks. "His philosophy was that you should concentrate on earnings-per-share growth and sales growth. He said if you can cover those two, you can do very well. So, if a company grows at 15 per cent a year, and you buy it at a fair price, your investment will grow at least 15 per cent a year. But Dobson's philosophy was to find companies that grew at 20 per cent plus. The '20 per cent plus' means that you double your money every three and a half years. That was his aim."

It was not always an approach for the faint of heart, but Formula Growth made it work. "If you can find one super stock out of every four stocks you buy, boy you're going to make it rich," says Catafago. "One stock is going to be terrible. Two will do nothing. But that one super stock will make up for everything else."

René Catafago regrets that he never had Dobson's patience in his own personal investing. "In Dobson's era, you had to buy a $1 stock and try to keep it as long as you could. Buy and hold from 1975 to 2000 was the only thing you could do, unless you were lucky and got out in 1987, not to come back until 1991. That was a terrible period of time. But buy and hold was a way to make money. I would have been way better off had I listened to Dobson's approach, because I had some stocks personally that I sold so early, thinking I was smart, and then they went up tenfold after I sold them."

Everyone agrees that Dobson had an extraordinary level of risk tolerance. "He always said that the big mistakes we made were mistakes of "omission," not "commission," says Ian Soutar. "The thing that really would upset us was missing a Wal-Mart at the early stage, not investing in something that went down 50 or 60 per cent. We wanted to make sure that everything was going to turn out to be an exceptional long-term growth opportunity. We'd look at them all. Sometimes we didn't like it – too expensive or we didn't like the people – and it would go on to be a success. Then we'd be really upset! John encouraged us to go out and take risks and do unconventional things. Those things that are often perceived as risky have the most opportunity."

A willingness to take on risk did not mean that Formula Growth was reckless. In fact, it was highly disciplined with its target sheets, used to assess potential stock purchases as well as to track a stock's ongoing performance. After attending a conference or visiting a company, the team would always go through the sheets carefully. "I remember one night we came back from San Francisco, Bette Lou [Reade], John, and I," recalls Soutar. "John insisted, because we hadn't done the worksheets yet, that we had to do them. So, we went to my house, and my wife was upstairs with our young children. We'd had a lot of drinks on the airplane, and we were making a lot of noise getting the worksheets done. And my wife was pretty upset about it. But that was John. You had to get the worksheets done."

Formula Growth usually tracked scores of stocks for potential purchase, and when there were not many stocks that were deemed to have a lot of potential, it was usually a sign that the market was too high, Soutar notes. "At those times, someone like Bette Lou [Reade] would suggest raising a little cash. But John never wanted cash in the portfolio, so he'd say to find stuff with potential. That sometimes perhaps led us to be a little more liberal when it came to assessing earnings." In short, Formula Growth was sometimes less rigid in its investing approach than other companies were.

Dobson was an optimist who believed that when he bought a company, he was buying its management as well. "His attitude," says former portfolio manager Kim Holden, "is that you're not renting the shares in the company. You are owning them and helping management in their endeavour to grow larger. He was very loyal. He tended to hold on to his investments and disregard the short-term negatives because he had such a long term-time horizon."

Dobson believed that management teams were the driving force behind a successful company, and that the best way to judge them was to meet face to face. "We want to see the whites of their eyes and gauge their desire to be successful and rich with their stock. Because if they get rich as shareholders, so will we," Dobson said. Senior officers of small companies usually have a significant portion of their net worth in their company and are often falling over themselves to get their story out. There is far more information available in this segment of the market when compared with large-cap companies, which are usually efficiently valued. Furthermore, the CEO of a large corporation like GE may never be available.

"Generally speaking, *Wall Street* covers only larger companies, and by investigating the company ourselves, we can find out information that few other people know, giving us an advantage," noted Dobson. "Because of our experience, judgment, and instincts, we can make quick decisions and buy these stocks at cheap valuations before the growth prospects are clear or widely known."

Formula Growth's large and varied network also allows it to triple- and quadruple-check information on a particular company. "There are many smart people on the sell side [brokerage/analysis/investment bankers] and the buy side [money managers]," said Dobson. By using all the available resources, Formula Growth developed an overall database of information that few other firms could rival.

Dobson was always a very patient investor, which sometimes cost Formula Growth dearly. "Sure, he rode some stocks to zero," says Ian Soutar. "But if you look at the money that John made, he did incredibly well by hanging on to things. John's instincts were usually very good about people and opportunities. He was very inarticulate in terms of explaining exactly what he was doing. But when you look at the track record of the guy, he was usually right and quite often early."

Dobson proudly stated that Formula Growth was always trying to hit home runs, shooting for the fences. "We've had a lot of winners over time, like WebMD (the Internet-based health information service). We bought that in a private deal with a company called Actamed, and they got merged with WebMD, also in a private deal. We had paid $1.73 for that, and it came public at $8, and within eight months, it went to $120 or so, although we sold most of it in the vicinity of $35 or $40. That's twenty-five times your money!

One of Formula Growth's most successful investments was in Hospital Corp. of America (HCA) of Nashville, one of the world's largest private operators of health care facilities. According to HCA Chairman Thomas J. Frist, Ian Soutar's Pembroke Management was the first institution to buy HCA stock when it went public in 1969. At that time, Soutar also introduced Dr Frist to Dobson and Formula Growth. Frist credits Formula Growth for opening doors to other money managers in Canada. Dobson and Soutar were also close to Jack Massey, who founded HCA with Frist's father.

Another good example of a successful Formula Growth investment was Service Merchandise, a Tennessee-based catalogue retail company founded by Raymond Zimmerman. Zimmerman first got to know Dobson, Ian Soutar, and Alex Hammond-Chambers at a meeting in Nashville, arranged through Jack Massey of Hospital Corp. As the company's sales soared, Formula Growth went on to be a big investor in Service Merchandise in the 1970s and 1980s. "We would talk frequently," says Zimmerman. "John would call me, or I would call him for his opinion, which I very much valued. He was a wonderful shareholder and a wonderful friend." (Service Merchandise went bankrupt in the late 1990s, but well after Formula Growth had sold its holding at a huge profit. Zimmerman later bought the former company's name and logo at an auction and has revived it as an online-only Web store.)

Raymond Zimmerman passed along some practical advice to his Canadian friends for assessing a company. One day, he got a call from Dobson saying that he, along with Ian Soutar and Alex Hammond-Chambers, planned to visit a Kentucky-based restaurant chain called Long John Silver's that specialized in seafood. "I told them that if the restroom is clean, then it's a pretty good store," Zimmerman recalls. "So the first thing they do when we get to Long John Silver's is go to the restroom to check out if it's a good place. I told them to look at the ladies' room because the men's room is easier to keep clean. It was around lunch time, and the restroom was a disaster. They all looked at each other and said, 'We're not buying stock here, or eating here!' A couple of months later, all the executives of the restaurant's parent company died in a plane crash, and the company went straight down. After that, I became their unofficial fast-food analyst."

A Dobson Investment Primer: Ten Guidelines

Formula Growth's ability to pick winners is the culmination of its disciplined investment approach, one that has remained virtually unchanged since the Fund's inception in 1960. It has rigorously championed several basic investment guidelines that have served its unit holders well.

Guideline #1: Let Compounding Work for You.

A line sometimes attributed to Albert Einstein goes as follows: "The greatest invention in human history is compound interest." Compounding is the ability to generate returns that are then reinvested and then generate their own returns. The power of compounding is truly magical over time. For example, the initial price of a Formula Growth unit was $9 in 1960 (at a time when the Canadian dollar was roughly at par with the US dollar). The founders invested approximately $10,000 each. Today, more than fifty years later, that $10,000, at a compound growth rate of more than 12.9 per cent per year (through 30 September 2013), would be worth over $6 million US (net of fees). By comparison, if the compounded growth rate had been the 9.9 per cent recorded by the S&P 500 index, a unit would have been worth just $1.5 million today.

Guideline #2: Buy Growth Stocks.

Dobson has long believed that the most important single rule is to buy a company with increasing earnings per share. This usually requires fast sales growth and a high return on equity to finance the growth. These factors are more often found in small emerging growth companies because their potential is greater than larger ones. Cyclicals are generally avoided because they are too hard to judge. Formula Growth also avoids stocks with high price-earnings (P/E) ratios. Twenty-five times earnings is generally the maximum tolerated.

Guideline #3: Usually Ignore Dividends.

Formula Growth believes a growth company should have better use for its money than paying dividends. If it does not have a better use for its money, that means the internal growth rate of the company is probably slowing down. So it is best to move on to another stock.

Guideline #4: Don't Be Deceived by Appearances.

Look at the individual company rather than starting with an industry approach. Recognize that mundane companies can do as well or better than glamorous ones. Frequently, technological innovation and superior management lead to big gains in unglamorous companies. Often, they can be bought at cheaper prices because of lack of investor interest and can become big winners.

Guideline #5: Trust People.

People are key. Portfolio managers and a company's management should preferably have a financial interest in the stock recommended. Ownership of Formula Growth has been in the hands of insiders since the 1970s, so its closely held shares trade at a cheap book value. This allows for flexibility with bonus payouts and the ability to attract talent. Never forget that success is about attracting, developing, and working with the best people.

Guideline #6: Be Patient.

Patience is very important. It is a serious error for an investor, upon retirement at age sixty-five, to decide to sell equities and move to yield (bonds, etc.). Retirees should continue to invest in equities and sell off a few shares as cash is needed.

Guideline #7: Stick to Your Niche.

Be consistent and disciplined, and do not switch strategies midstream. Minimize attention to short-term considerations, and remain fully invested. Otherwise, investors can lose too much on market turns and miss out on big potential gains because of short-term worries. Missing the best ten days in a bull market move means missing out on 80 per cent of the upside move. Never try to time the market.

Guideline #8: Be Prepared to Make Mistakes. Diversification Is Key.

Investors can never be 100 per cent sure about any investment. That is why there are always buyers and sellers. In a fast-moving world with modern technology, it is essential to diversify risk and incubate portfolio holdings. Always be prepared to make mistakes, and do not dwell on them.

Guideline #9: Develop a Strong Network.

The development and proper use of an information network, good market intelligence, and useful contacts, especially among fellow fund managers if one is in that business, are all equally important. For comfort, get to know somebody local who has good knowledge of the people running a given company.

> ## Guideline #10: Limit Sales and Marketing (If You Are Running a Fund).
>
> Do not spend too much time on sales and marketing. These activities steal time from the work of the best stock pickers because clients always want to meet them. If you limit hours spent on marketing, more time is freed up for investment analysis.

∞ FINDING THE TRUE VALUE ∞

Formula Growth has always believed that small-cap investing is the best avenue for getting the highest returns in the long run. In doing so, it often looks for what it calls an "earnings growth and multiple expansion double play." This is the significant acceleration a stock price gets with having growing earnings and a growing multiple. For example, a $15 stock trading at a multiple valuation of fifteen with earnings growth of 20 per cent will grow to $18, assuming the same valuation. However, if the multiple increases to twenty, what results is a $24 stock, and the return will increase from 20 per cent to 60 per cent. That kind of growth in stock price is easier when a company is small and relatively unknown when you buy in.

When evaluating a stock, Formula Growth gives some thought to the impact of macroeconomic factors and to the P/E ratio. But it devotes much more time and effort to determining the growth rate of an individual company. "At the end of the day, we believe that growth pushes the P/E multiple," explained Dobson. "We essentially look at the business, estimate a growth rate for three to five years, and apply a reasonable multiple to it. We can then determine the price a stock could trade at over the next few years and conclude whether it is a sound investment or not."

Despite these calculations, in Dobson's view, investing is often more of an art than a science. "There is no mathematical equation that can be applied to the stock market and yield precise results. Experience and judgment are an investor's best friend."

Misjudgment by investors of the "real value" of businesses is one of the major sources of disappointment in stocks, leading investors to overpay. In the growth-stock universe, the obsession with short-term earnings growth and relative valuation leads to superficial analysis. "We strongly believe that the short term does not matter. One needs to be mindful that it is a series of short terms that add up to the long term," said Dobson. "Volatility in the market is generally a result of too many people focusing on what will happen in three months, rather than on where a company will be in three years."

In the long run, day-to-day changes in the stock price tend to be dwarfed by the overall trends. A large stock price change may be significant today but only a blip in five years if the stock has continued to grow. "This volatility is actually an advantage to us because when other people are selling in a mad panic, stocks are on sale," Dobson said. "A stock that may have been too expensive before can suddenly be cheaply priced and perfect to be bought, assuming the core story is intact."

Formula Growth analysts look at several characteristics of a company in order to gauge the growth prospects and determine an appropriate valuation. After first assessing the growth rate of earnings and sales, they study the company's market cap relative to the scope of the business opportunity, the competitive environment, the nature of the business and whether it is cyclical or has recurring revenue, whether the firm is capital intensive or not, the growth dynamics of customers, operating leverage, dependence upon capital markets for growth plans, and return on invested capital.

∞ CATCHING A FALLING KNIFE ∞

Dobson cautioned that there were always pitfalls in investing that should be avoided. "We try to avoid catching up to a hot sector and investing in the 'old winners' when there is probably nowhere left to go but down." Trying to justify valuations by comparing a stock to other stocks that have very high multiples can also be a mistake, he said. The fact that similar companies have higher or lower multiples should be only one element you need to consider when valuing a stock. Moreover, being inflexible or having a "hard head" is a brutal character flaw in an investor. "Not realizing when you are wrong torpedoes an investment portfolio." This behavior usually leads to averaging down or buying more stock at lower levels, which is hazardous if not done with care. "It can be likened to catching a falling knife," said Dobson. "It's hard to time it just right." He cautioned against playing "hot tips" because, generally, these stocks have already had great runs.

Sadly, many investors do not have the patience to see an idea through to fruition. They make a dollar or two and are excited to take profits and show how bright they are. "If you are in front of a good story, you must give it time to unfold," said Dobson. "That's how you make doubles or triples!"

Dobson also believed deeply that one of the most important ingredients for successful investing is optimism. "Pessimists will never make good investors because they cannot look at the short-term uncertainties in a company and see the pot of gold beyond it. The only companies pessimists feel comfortable investing in are those that are without flaws. The problem is there is nowhere to go but down as these stocks are priced for perfection."

Investors must also be conscious of the fact that for every death, there is a birth. For example, IBM's loss of its dominant market share was Microsoft's gain. Hard work and passion are also vital because finding "the next big thing" takes time. "If you can't get up in the morning and look forward to your day, then you will not be the one kicking over that one special stone and finding the next Wal-Mart," said Dobson. "There will always be a company that is growing. You just have to find it and see it for what it could be. Remember, Sam Walton started with just one store."

Dobson's Top Eight Investment Criteria

The Formula Growth team has always tried to buy shares in a company at an early point in its life cycle, when revenues and profits are ascending swiftly. Here are some of the criteria they look for:

1. **Revenue Growth:** Sales gains should be steady. This tells you that the company has successfully tapped a need or niche in the marketplace. Does the company also operate in a growing market for its goods or services?

2. **Earnings-Per-Share Growth:** Rapid revenue and earnings growth do not always equal big profits. What counts is how much a company can bring to the bottom line on a per-share basis. Solid profits allow companies to finance their own expansion.

3. **Price-Earnings (P/E) Ratio:** This measure represents the stock price divided by the current year's forecast earnings per share. Ideally, it should be about half the earnings growth rate. The P/E ratio is essentially the reflecting pool for all of the information in the public marketplace (including interest rates and inflation), incorporating investors' expectations for growth and the risk associated with it. A key to growth-stock investing is to understand or develop a feel for what the three-to-five-year P/E should be.

4. **Price-Sales Ratio:** This is the stock price divided by per-share sales. Companies with high sales volumes and low profit margins should be around one time. Companies with proprietary products and high margins should be around three times.

5. **Accounting:** Practices should be conservative. Revenues should be booked when they are received, and expenses recognized when incurred.

6. **Momentum:** Formula Growth does not worry about catching a stock at a low. Instead, it looks for stocks that are outperforming at least 80 per cent of the market. Relative strength in a stock means investors are coming around to your idea. It is also important to know whether the stock is in a leading group or sector of the stock market.

7. **Balance Sheet:** This should be healthy. Debt can limit a company's ability to conduct research and development, launch new products, fight competitors, or get through tough economic times.

8. **Margins:** Are margins high or low? This indicates the degree of leadership or proprietorship the company has in its industry. Pay attention to the trend. Are margins rising or falling? Formula Growth often prefers lower margins because companies that start with high margins likely have nowhere to go but down.

CHAPTER 8

Case Studies: It's All About Growth

*One good management team and investment can lead
you right to the next one. Don't miss it.*

— JOHN DOBSON

In John Dobson's view, superior growth rates in companies can typically be broken down into four different buckets of opportunity:

1. Innovation/Discovery
2. Unit Growth in a Growth Industry
3. Market Share Growth in a Mature Industry
4. Consolidation/Acquisition Strategies

Over the years, stocks in the Formula Growth portfolio often fell into one or more of the above four buckets. The "best of the best" are companies that are in the second category: exhibiting unit growth in a growth industry. Fast, well-executed growth usually results in margin expansion as increasing scale pushes the business model into a "sweet spot," where incremental revenue dollars contribute higher profit margins. This phenomenon is called "operating leverage."

"Because many costs in a business are fixed, increasing sales over a given level where fixed costs are fully absorbed allows for more gross margin to fall to the bottom line," explains Formula Growth president Randy Kelly. "The beauty of this phenomenon from a stock perspective is that it generally leads to P/E (price/earnings) expansion and a large upward re-rating in the stock price."

Formula Growth likens this to winning the exacta at the race-track, explains Kelly. "Quickly growing earnings per share (EPS), with a rising P/E multiple, results in very large stock price moves." Other features of the best stocks involve limited growth in the number of shares outstanding, which means there is very little dilution to earnings per share. "More often than not, Formula Growth would find the stocks that fell into these four buckets before the public had caught on to the story," notes Kelly.

At times, this lack of public interest was due to the company being controversial or hard to understand. Sometimes, the market was in a bearish phase, and investors were simply not buying anything, let alone unknown quantities. In other cases, it was because the company was a little small or had too short a track record and therefore was ignored by Wall Street analysts. Inevitably, the company's attractiveness would become more obvious, and its Wall Street coverage improved. With that would come a higher profile and a higher stock price as other investors jumped on board.

The following case studies, all major winners for Formula Growth, illustrate at least one of the four characteristics in successful stocks that were, or still are, part of Formula Growth's investment portfolio.

∞ CIRCUIT CITY: ∞
UNIT GROWTH IN A GROWING MARKET

In the early 1980s, John Dobson found himself travelling in Florida on a series of company visits with Dick Lilly, an analyst with Tampa Bay-based investment dealer Raymond James. They decided to pop in on the Florida outlets of Circuit City, a Virginia-based retailer then known as Wards Company, which had been founded in 1949 by Sam Wurtzel. Dobson was impressed by what he saw. His instincts told him something big was going on with this emerging company. (Wards was completely unrelated to another legendary US retailer, Montgomery Ward, which later went out of business. In fact, the name "Wards" was simply an acronym composed of the founder's last initial and those of his wife and sons – W = Wurtzel; A = Alan; R = Ruth; D = David; S = Sam.)

Circuit City pioneered "big-box" retailing in the 1970s and 1980s and ended up becoming the second-largest consumer electronics retailer in the United States, with 567 Circuit City Superstores at its peak. These stores represented a revolution in how televisions and other consumer electronics, as well as large appliances, were sold. When Dobson purchased his first shares of Wards, at what later ended up as a split-adjusted price of pennies a share, he knew he was buying into a solid growth company that had plans to expand retail square footage aggressively by building greenfield (new) locations or acquiring existing stores and rebranding them as Circuit City Superstores. The thinking was that this expansion would drive earnings per share higher, and the stock price would follow.

What was not obvious at the time, even to Dick Lilly and Dobson, was the coming boom in consumer electronic devices that were being developed following technological breakthroughs in the semiconductor industry. Typical of these new products was the mass-market video cassette recorder (VCR). VCRs first made their appearance in the 1960s and 1970s, but the devices were expensive and difficult to use, making them more of a curiosity than a mainstream consumer product. But by the early 1980s, companies such as Sony, JVC, and Toshiba leveraged new low-cost technology to turn the VCR into a consumer-friendly household item. Content suddenly became available thanks to the burgeoning sales of video cassettes and the growth of rental providers such as Blockbuster Entertainment, another great stock once owned by Formula Growth.

Before long, household penetration of the VCR in America was over 90 per cent. The initial high price points associated with this kind of revolutionary product allowed for strong margins for both manufacturers and retailers. Randy Kelly still recalls that his first bonus from Formula Growth was a VCR from JVC that cost a whopping $1,500. Dobson insisted that the device would be a boon to the perpetually busy Kelly, who would now be able to "time shift" the business shows on TV that Dobson insisted he should not miss.

With the rollout of other devices like PCs, CD players, pagers, high-definition TVs, and cellphones, Circuit City went on to become one of the best performing stocks on the NYSE, after graduating to the senior exchange in 1984 from NASDAQ. With high prices, fat margins, and growing square footage, Circuit City's earnings per share took off, and Formula Growth won the "exacta." Because Wall Street did not hear of Wards until much later, Dobson was able to pick up the stock at P/E multiples below ten. Formula Growth watched the stock take flight as the Street belatedly discovered the name, and the multiple in time more than doubled. Initial positions in the stock were purchased at less than $0.25 a share, and the stock went on to top out at $40 a share. Formula made 100 times on its investment and owned the stock for about twenty years.

Like all good things, the Circuit City story eventually had to end. Competition came to the big-box consumer electronics stores with the arrival of Best Buy and several other serious competitors. Circuit City discovered that its real estate locations were now subpar by comparison, and that its store designs were looking stale. At the same time, margins dropped precipitously as manufacturers found new ways to add features and cut prices to stimulate demand. In the end, gross margins on TVs ended up in the single-digit range.

Circuit City tried to compensate for this collapse in retail margins by attaching extended warranty contracts to a range of its products. But this proved too little, too late, and the company had no choice but to liquidate in 2009. Fortunately, by then, Formula Growth was long out of the stock.

A happy side note to the Circuit City story is the 2002 spinoff to shareholders of the company's CarMax Inc. subsidiary. Circuit City executives had founded CarMax in 1993, believing that the skill sets they had honed as big-box retailers of electronic products and appliances would be well suited to the fragmented market for used cars. They were right. Today, CarMax is the largest publicly traded retailer of used cars, with sales of over $10 billion annually and a market capitalization of over $10 billion. And Formula Growth still owns some shares in CarMax.

As Dobson frequently said as he coached his team, "One good management team and investment can lead you right to the next one. Don't miss it."

FIGURE 8.1: CIRCUIT CITY

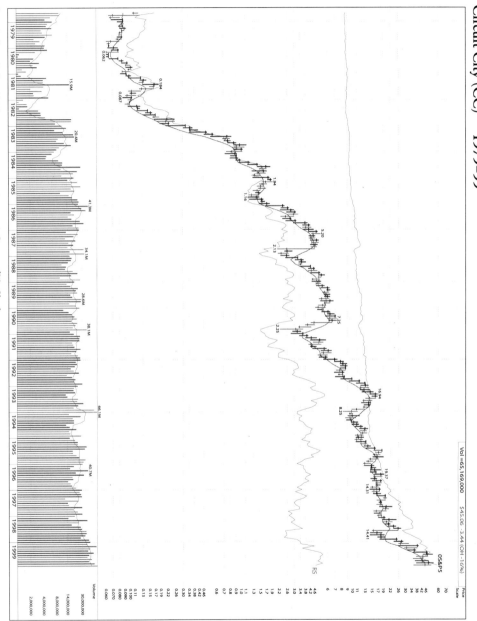

Circuit City (CC)   1979–99

∞ CELGENE: ∞
INNOVATION, DISCOVERY, AND PERSISTENCE

Celgene Corporation is a biopharmaceutical company engaged in the discovery, development, and commercialization of new drugs for the treatment of cancer and immunological diseases. Founded as a spinoff from Celanese Corporation, the US chemicals giant, it went public in 1987 through the legendary West Coast broker and banker Hambrecht & Quist, with whom Formula Growth had a long-term relationship.

Celgene's initial focus was on specialty chemical products and bio-remediation materials used to clean up toxic wastes. It also aimed to develop lightweight, high-strength polymers for a range of uses through a technology known as biocatalysis. But these businesses went nowhere until the company decided to make a dramatic shift, propelling it to become a major pharmaceutical company and a terrific stock.

In the late 1990s, Celgene licensed thalidomide from New York's Rockefeller University, helping to revive a drug that had become a pariah decades earlier. Thalidomide was introduced in the late 1950s as an anti-nausea drug to help pregnant women deal with the effects of morning sickness. But it was withdrawn from worldwide sale in 1962 after being found to cause birth defects.

Despite its removal from the market, thalidomide remained the subject of significant clinical interest and research. Convinced of its potential for treatment of ailments as diverse as cancer and AIDS, Celgene licensed the use of thalidomide from Rockefeller and began to develop a pipeline of anti-cancer drugs.

Formula Growth's Kim Holden, working closely with Bob Power, a one-time Hambrecht & Quist broker who had landed at New Orleans-based Southcoast Capital, built a position in Celgene in the late 1990s at a split-adjusted average price of $1.50 a share. The idea was to participate with the company as it sought approval from the US Food and Drug Administration (FDA) for its innovative approach to an old compound that had been left to fallow.

By 2001, the company had two products in the market: Thalomid® and Focalin®. Thalomid (thalidomide) was used for indications of leprosy, although with strict protocols to ensure that pregnant women were excluded. Importantly, Thalomid was also being widely used off-label (i.e., prescribed for uses other than what the FDA has approved) in cases of multiple myeloma and other forms of cancer. The growing off-label use and eventual success of Thalomid was exactly what Formula Growth was looking for, and it held on for the ride as Thalomid was further refined into a new drug called Revlimid®. Focalin was licensed to Novartis and is used to treat attention deficit disorder (ADD).

Celgene continues to build on its oncology and auto-immune businesses and retains its strategy of making acquisitions to expand its technology portfolio and distribution capabilities. Though Formula Growth has sold much of its position in Celgene over the years, it still owns some stock, which has increased in value by seventy times.

FIGURE 8.2: CELEGENE

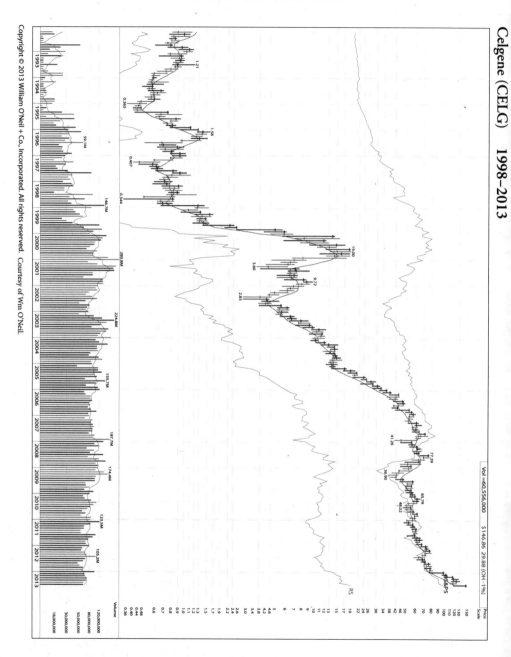

Celgene (CELG) 1998–2013

∽ HOME DEPOT: EXPANSION AND INNOVATION ∾

When Formula Growth first invested in Home Depot in the 1980s, it was an obscure Atlanta-based retailer, a long way from being the world's largest home improvement chain. John Lowenberg from Robinson Humphrey, one of Formula Growth's network of contacts in Atlanta, thought highly of Home Depot's management, its innovative concept, and its growth prospects. He convinced Dobson to visit an early Home Depot store. Seeing first-hand the reality behind the story, Dobson bought Home Depot's stock at the time of the initial public offering (IPO) in 1981 and watched it run up twenty times in the next couple of years. He then sold and was out of the stock by 1983. Again, the discipline of Formula Growth's price target sheets correctly exited the firm out of what had become an expensive stock.

The timing was fortunate as it was not long after that the Home Depot made an ill-fated acquisition of the Bowater Home Centers chain, which turned out more difficult to assimilate than first thought. Given this disappointment, and its already-expensive valuation, Home Depot's stock price dropped by two-thirds by the beginning of 1986.

Those three years in purgatory corrected the stock's egregious valuation, and Formula Growth again began to build a position. By the 1980s, management had fine-tuned the Home Depot big-box retail concept and went on to methodically expand its presence throughout the United States. The larger Home Depot became, the more merchandise it would buy, and the better prices it would get from suppliers. Instead of keeping these improved margins, the company chose to pass the savings on to its customers. This virtuous circle of ever-lower prices and higher sales obliterated the competition and grew Home Depot's market share exponentially.

Home Depot's cross-country rollout was perfectly timed to coincide with the growth of the American public's love affair with the do-it-yourself concept. Home Depot CEO Bernie Marcus and his

team soon found that the company's stores were always full of customers. While management appreciated the profitability of the busy
stores, they knew the customer experience was suffering. As a result,
Home Depot would always err on the side of plowing more capital
into opening new stores, even when those outlets initially cannibal-
ized sales from existing stores, confident that the end result would
squeeze more sales out of an existing market. Even though this use
of company capital did not always please Wall Street, management
was convinced that this combination of deeper market penetration
and broader market share was building a moat around the business.

By the end of the 1980s, Home Depot was once again the dar-
ling of the investing public, and over the next decade, its valuation
ran far ahead of the stock. By 1999, shares were selling at seventy
times next year's earnings, clearly an unsustainable level. With stock
bought at a split-adjusted price of 50 cents a share trading at $70 in
1999, Formula Growth had sold much of its position, scoring a hun-
dred-fold gain. With a high P/E ratio and a faltering decade ahead for
the US stock market and economy, it was inevitable that the Home
Depot stock would be in for a tough time. Twice during the 2000s,
the stock touched $20 a share as growth slowed substantially. Yet
Home Depot has continued to demonstrate its old resilience and has
again come back strong. In 2013, the company surpassed its old high
of $70 a share.

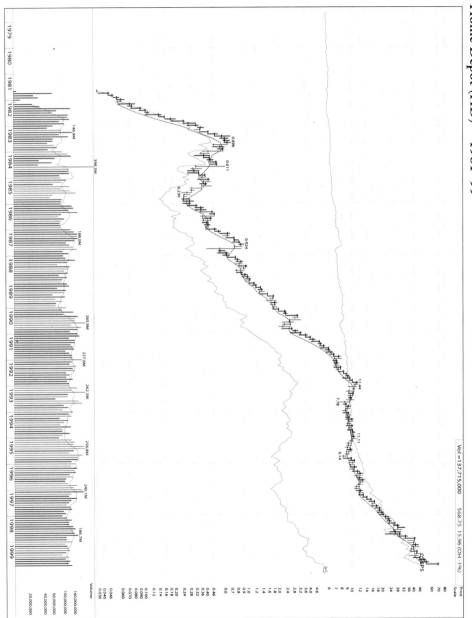

FIGURE 8.3: HOME DEPOT

∞ CALLAWAY GOLF CO.: ∞
WALL STREET COVERAGE, INNOVATION, AND MARKETING

This was one instance where Dobson did not need any help understanding what the company was making. He could pick it up and swing it! Callaway Golf, which went public in 1992, was all about the Big Bertha driver, which used the latest technology to revolutionize the design of drivers and build a product that became the top of its class.

Formula Growth was aware of the company because Randy Kelly was playing with a Callaway driver, and it was obvious to him that the product was different and better than anything else available. Formula Growth's long association with the game of golf meant that the firm had a solid network of pros, retailers, and competitors who were not reluctant to share their opinions on anything related to the game. Dobson, who helped to run the Canadian Open a couple of times, thought Kelly was nuts to pay a large amount of money for a single club. What was less obvious at the time was that the company's founder, Ely Callaway Jr, was a brilliant marketer. To Callaway, it mattered little what the product was – it was all in the positioning. He had already been successful in marketing wine from his own vineyards, so golf clubs could not be any harder. He convinced Formula Growth of his business plan to build the Callaway brand on the back of "Big Bertha" and extend it further into other golf equipment.

Yet the high price set in Callaway's IPO turned off plenty of investors, and the stock drifted in its first six months of trading, partially because of this skepticism, but also because it soon emerged that GE Capital, an early investor in the firm when it was still private, wanted to sell its large position. This put a lid on the stock price until a secondary offering was organized and cleared GE out of the firm.

Formula Growth was shut out of the secondary offering by the lead investment banker but was able to accumulate stock quickly before and after the deal in the aftermarket at comparable prices. This proved to be a lucky break, since it soon became clear that the business was exploding, just as Ely had promised. Callaway became the first major golf brand, and for five years, was the only brand to own. True to its plan, the company diversified into irons, putters, bags, and balls through innovative product development and occasionally through acquisitions. Revenue growth and profitability were high, and Formula Growth's return on its investment increased fivefold in just four years.

It is inevitable that highly lucrative businesses eventually get replicated, and by 1996, several new companies with big marketing budgets had entered the golf market. While the golf industry is large, it is also fairly mature. Total rounds of golf played do not grow much year over year, and there has been no surge in participation in the sport. As a result, Callaway and its competitors remain locked in an expensive battle for market share. That sort of business environment is not the kind that interests Formula Growth any longer, and it has long since moved on.

FIGURE 8.4: CALLAWAY GOLF CO.

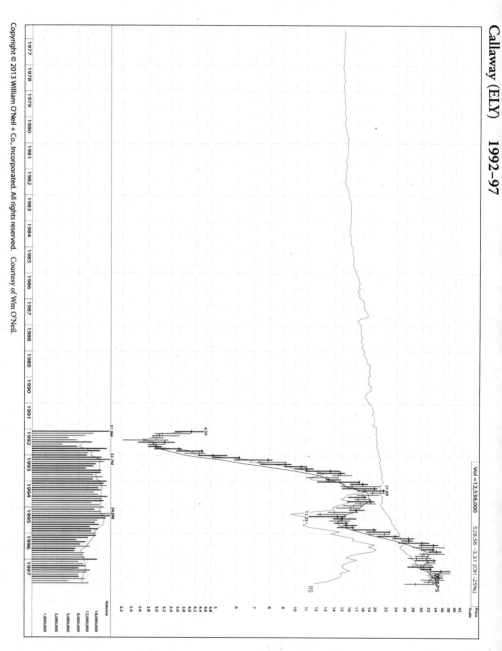

Callaway (ELY) 1992–97

∞ CISCO SYSTEMS: ∞
"CASTLE IN THE SKY" AND UNIT GROWTH

Being in the right place at the right time is the magical formula for quickly getting a big stock price increase. Formula Growth first noticed Cisco in 1990 after a hot IPO appeared where no one on the Street got as much stock as they wanted. The offering was priced at $18 a share, which works out to about 6 cents a share today after many splits over the past twenty plus years. The stock moved up quickly post-IPO but stalled when 1990 drew to a close as investors worried about the prospects of the Gulf War and its possible impact on the economy and corporate earnings.

Formula Growth struck quickly during the stock market malaise and loaded up on what it viewed as a quality player in a fast-growing industry at a reasonable earnings multiple. Formula Growth had been involved in networking companies like 3Com and knew that Cisco was a step ahead of the other players. What began as a technology investment in a company that was simply selling networking routers morphed into an incredible play on the subsequent Internet explosion. As the Internet expanded, Cisco's networking hardware started to fly off the shelves as the company supplied the routers and other equipment that kept the Internet going.

Investors began to make fanciful predictions that the Internet and the companies supplying software and hardware to it would have no bounds. During the 1990s, the logic was that if earnings and revenues for companies supplying the Internet were doubling each year and even each quarter, then surely these companies must be worth one hundred times those earnings. A "Castle in the Sky" was built, and enormous price tags were put on stocks like Cisco, which peaked at a P/E multiple of 154 in 2000, giving it a price of $80 a share and a market capitalization in excess of a cool $500 billion. (Castle in the Sky is a term coined by Burton Malkiel in his 1973 book *A Random Walk Down Wall Street*.) In keeping with its discipline on target prices, Formula Growth sold most of its stock by 2000 as the valuation marched ridiculously skyward, and the growth in revenues and earnings slowly came back to earth. Today, Cisco's value is about a quarter of that peak.

FIGURE 8.5: CISCO SYSTEMS

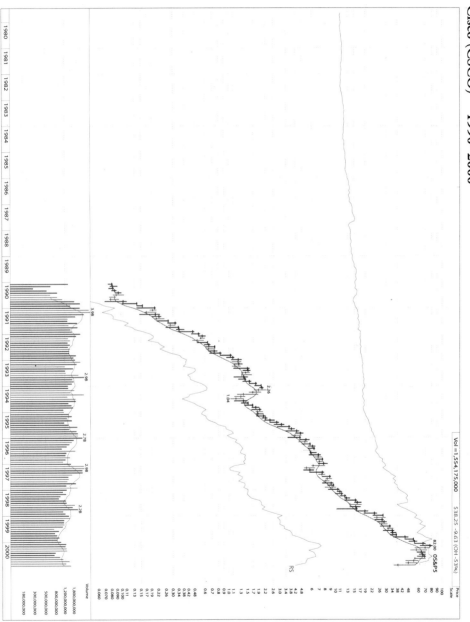

Cisco (CSCO)   1990–2000

◌◌ RENT-A-CENTER INC.: ◌◌
CONSOLIDATION, POOR CREDIT, AND HIGH RETURNS

Founding a business designed to serve customers with low-paying jobs and poor credit histories may not seem like the easiest way to attract investors. However, Rent-A-Center (RAC), which provides low-income consumers with rent-to-own options for acquiring furniture and appliances, was able to beautifully execute its strategy of growing its store base and penetrating the market to build an extremely successful business. The company has grown from sixteen stores to over 3000 since its IPO in 1995. Its revenues have increased twenty-fold.

When a business seems illogical or just too tough to pull off, many investors will shy away from the opportunity and will instead chase "the next big thing," even if it is expensively valued. Rent-A-Center is the kind of company that prompts you to wonder how management does it, but its longevity demonstrates that success is possible.

At first glance, it seems crazy to allow consumers with low incomes and no bank accounts to walk out of your store with big-ticket appliances, televisions, and furniture. But Rent-A-Center has the systems and management to handle this tricky business. On the front end of the initial rental transaction, Rent-A-Center gauges the stability of the customer by using references, pre-existing relationships, and other methods. On the back end, the company knows that it can cost-effectively repossess the goods if necessary and quickly get them back out on rental to earn a return. Most importantly, the nature of the pricing of its weekly rental contracts allows for sufficient profit margin to compensate for the intricate micro-lending business Rent-A-Center is essentially running. With solid margins and the fact that each piece of merchandise will likely be rented out three to four times to different clients, the company can earn a healthy return on equity and generate strong cash flows.

Over the years, Formula Growth has had big successes with public companies such as Rent-A-Center, which operate in what might be termed as America's "shadow banking system." The portfolio has included companies that sell used cars to sub-prime consumers, collection companies, sub-prime credit card issuers, and non-conventional lenders like pawn shops.

Recently, Internet-based micro-lending has been growing quickly, and Formula Growth has a few holdings in that space. While upfront credit losses may be heavy, they are more than offset by far lower loan origination costs. Industry experts estimate that as many as 20 per cent of US consumers are "unbanked" today, and that percentage is staying constant. The mainstream banks do not want to deal with this customer segment and push them away by charging steep fees for cheque writing, NSF cheques, and everything else under the sun. In this landscape, Rent-A-Center has done a great job of putting most of its competitors out of business, giving the company a large market that it continues to penetrate.

FIGURE 8.6: RENT-A-CENTER INC.

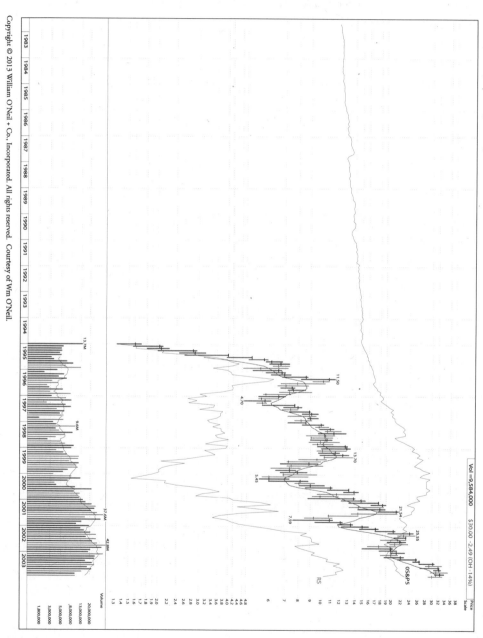

CHAPTER 9

Boom and Bust

The 1990s were a golden era for stocks and for
Formula Growth. The 2000s, not so much.

— RANDY KELLY

Formula Growth entered the 1990s in trouble: it had difficulty marketing its funds and faced a high level of redemptions from unhappy investors. "By 1990, nothing's going right," says Randy Kelly. "We're getting fired by our institutional accounts. The pensions are under water just like today, and we're getting reallocated out. We're losing customers by the boatload. It's looking bad."

The stock markets were hard hit by a recession in the United States that lasted from July 1990 to March 1991. It was the deepest recession since the early 1980s and contributed to George H.W. Bush's re-election defeat in 1992. Although mainly attributable to the workings of the business cycle and to restrictive monetary policy, the 1990–91 recession demonstrated the growing importance of financial markets to the American and world economies. The Iraqi invasion of Kuwait in August 1990 also played a role, causing the Dow to drop 18 per cent in three months, from 2,911.63 on 3 July, to 2,381.99 on 16 October.

However, over the long term, the first Gulf War helped fuel a subsequent market boom. "This was kind of the catalyst the market needed," says Kelly. "And, as proof, we started to go up sharply. In 1991, we were up over 70 per cent. In 1992 and 1993, we gained over 25 per cent. In 1994, we were flat, but in 1995, we were up another 37 per cent. And then the Internet boom took off for another leg of big increases."

In fact, from the end of 1990 to 2000, when you include the effect of the strengthening US dollar, a unit of Formula Growth Fund went from about $380 to $5,400 in Canadian dollars, and Dobson was once again a hero to unit holders. "Everybody loved Dobson in a way because he was a genius," says René Catafago. "The genius was that he had made so many people wealthy over the years. When you look at Formula Growth, a unit that was $9 at inception went up to $5,400 in a matter of about forty years. That's a huge return!"

Randy Kelly says the 1990s were a great decade for Formula Growth because it was heavily weighted to technology stocks, which took off with the Internet boom. "We were off to the races again. Kind of like 1975–83, the period 1991–95 was great. There was lots of volatility. But that's not bad when the direction is mostly up and to the right. The markets were on fire, and there was a birthing of a whole bunch of great stories, like the emergence of the first browser, Netscape. Every telecom company had to start rewiring. Cellulars were birthing. It was a good time to be a growth investor again. By the end of the decade, the NASDAQ hit a record 5000."

⨀ A NEW PLAYER COMES ON BOARD ⨀

A new player entered the world of Formula Growth during this period: John Liddy, who is now executive vice-president based in New York. Liddy was working at Midland Walwyn as an analyst covering Canadian stocks when, in October 1994, he met Dobson and Randy Kelly after giving an address at an Acorn Society dinner in Montreal. The Acorn Society was a small, informal group of Montreal portfolio managers and analysts who would meet occasionally to hear from visiting CEOs and others in the field of finance. Founded in 1975 by a group that included Ian Soutar, it kept up its periodic meetings until 1997. "They spoke to Pembroke Management to help pick candidates for a new portfolio manager," Liddy recalls. "I had never heard of Formula Growth because they managed only US stocks and didn't have much of a relationship with the Canadian brokerage community."

John Liddy met with Dobson, Randy Kelly, and Bette Lou Reade and heard the Formula Growth story for the first time. "Their terrific investment record got me interested, and I joined five months later. There were only four staffers then, but they were growing. Their investment success was unlike anybody else's in Canada. They were working in the United States with very exciting companies and had incredible corporate success stories. They had owned Cisco since its 1991 IPO and Home Depot in 1988 at the dawn of big-box marketers."

Liddy said that what impressed him the most was that Dobson's main motivation was not the love of making money. "It was never a question of having returned 18 per cent versus 17.5 per cent. It was all about feeling that you're a participant in growth in these successful growth companies. That's what fired him up."

Liddy liked Formula Growth's approach, which was to invest in entrepreneurial companies led by their founders. "When we went to hear a story, the guy telling it was the founder," he says. "We'd be getting a real, personally driven energy level that's different from the corporate overseer level. This approach melded well with John's passion for interpersonal relationships. What John liked to do was make friends, and he was good at it. The basic premise is: who are these people, are they likely to be successful? Then he'd check around with his network. This is a fantastic way of investing – very primal, very straightforward."

Dobson's measure of success is the return he was able to deliver to his clients. "That was his 100 per cent preoccupation," says Liddy. "The greatest moment for John professionally would be when a golf pro who invested $10,000 back in the day said twenty-five years later, 'You've really done a wonderful job for me. Everything I have is thanks to what you did.' That, for John, is the exact goal he would have had."

In a note marking Dobson's eightieth birthday, the late MP Heward Grafftey said, "I originally invested $10,000 in Formula Growth, and within a year, my investment increased to $20,000.

With the profit, I built a swimming pool and tennis court at a new estate in the Eastern Townships. Much to John's amusement, I called it the 'Formula Growth Sports Complex.'"

John Liddy, who was only thirty when he joined Formula Growth, said his youth was never a shortcoming in Dobson's mind. "John's whole life had always been about interacting with young people who were starting a business, starting a life. That energy level was very appealing to him. He always acted as a mentor to younger staffers, giving them side projects, stocks he thought were interesting."

"We all travelled extremely intensively for investments," Liddy adds. "We were typically on the road twenty weeks a year. John had a nose in all industries in the United States that were on the cutting edge of making the economy interesting. He always operated within a universe of three degrees of separation – he knew so many people. He felt most comfortable if he could check somebody out personally. It's not about the numbers. It's much more about the people. His disappointment was thinking somebody's a good person and finding out that was not true."

Money management firms usually create a very difficult working environment. Those companies are highly competitive, Liddy explains, and staffed by people who are smart, aggressive, and opinionated. "My way to judge any money management firm is, 'Do people stick around or not?' Here, at Formula Growth, everybody sticks around. The number one thing John stood for was loyalty – friends and co-professionals. His band of friends and band of brothers were very important."

Liddy adds that while the portfolio management business is demanding, Dobson never allowed the demands of the business to infect the work culture at Formula Growth. "His philosophy was that business should be enjoyable, and you should have fun doing it. You should find things that work for you, improve society, and make money. He enjoyed the 'treasure hunt' part of this job. He thought that was fun and should be central."

Formula Growth has always competed against a thousand other groups, most of them much larger, but has managed to persevere for over half a century. "Professional money management has become a bit of a grey, boring business over the past twenty years," says Liddy. "John was an old-fashioned gunslinger. We like that here. He wanted to find the next thing that will make you ten times your money – that's why you come to the office."

John Liddy was born in Toronto, grew up in Ottawa, and worked in Toronto until he moved to Montreal in 1995 with his wife and three daughters, who are now teenagers. After thirteen years, during which the city enjoyed a resurgence, he moved to New York in 2008 to open an office for Formula Growth. "We could see more people and be closer to an important set of relations with brokers who cover us," he explains.

Liddy's vision is to gradually increase the firm's size without losing its essence. By 2013, the original Formula Growth Fund and the two hedge funds that were established in the new millennium had total assets of about $500 million. What makes Formula Growth unique, he notes, is that in an industry committed to rapid change, even after fifty years, its makeup and philosophy show a great continuity with the firm in earlier days.

After spectacular stock market results during the 1990s, the tech bubble burst around 2000. Formula Growth was better insulated than others because of its disciplined approach, but the market sell-off still hurt. "Fortunately, our discipline and our targeting wouldn't let us get into the grocery.coms and drugstore.coms because we thought they were garbage," says Kelly. "In 1999, we were in better tech companies with real businesses underlying them. We were in telecom service companies that serviced the Internet dot bombs. We were one step removed. But guess what happened? As the dot bombs unspooled, the whole thing imploded. So 2000, 2001, and 2002 were worse for us, and it was worse for everybody."

Formula Growth started coming back in 2003, but, overall, because of market breakdowns in 2000, 2002, and 2008, the entire decade was a slow one for the US market. "It was a tough period for American stocks, but Canadian stocks did extremely well because they were dominated by commodities," explains Randy Kelly. "That started to change in the second decade of the new millennium, when the US stock market began to once again hit new highs and the Canadian market dragged due to lower commodity prices."

René Catafago notes, "In the first decade of the 2000s, the United States has been steadily weakened with slow growth. It really started after the dot-com debacle when things blew up and people lost a lot of money. And then you had 9/11, and the government started to spend too much money for one reason or another and went to war. So the United States lost a lot of its clout. It was all very harmful to their capital markets. Now markets are recovering, but the biggest problem with the United States remains the fact that they have so much debt."

Printing money may be the only option for paying back that debt, which will lead to a lot of inflation, Catafago adds. "In this environment, one of the best places to hide would be stocks. Companies at least will have pricing power with inflation. If we go back to the best years of Formula Growth's existence, it was during high inflation years, between 1975 and 1982."

∞ FORMULA GROWTH HEDGES ITS BETS ∞

The dot-com debacle of 2000 prompted Formula Growth management to re-evaluate its approach, and for the first time in its forty-year history, consider broadening its investment offering. "Until then, Formula Growth had simply been a long-only (buy) shop investing in aggressive growth equities," explains Randy Kelly. "Given the inherent volatility in our long-only process, and with the culmination of the bubble stock valuations in the year 2000, we came to the conclusion that we needed to offer our clients a different and less-volatile product. We felt it important, and the clients were demanding a product that took less risk and therefore would have less volatility."

As a result of this, Formula Growth decided to develop a hedge fund platform. "We came up with a long/short equity fund where we avail ourselves of the same research process we use to buy stocks long but also use the same research to sell stocks short," explains John Liddy. "We sell stocks short when our research indicates that stories are unspooling and the stock is likely to decline."

Much of Formula Growth's focus since the end of 2002 has been on building out its long/short business. "Our Formula Growth Hedge Fund is a wonderful complement to our long-only business or the original Formula Growth Fund," says Kelly. "The fact that we've been able to do this is a tribute to John Dobson's outstanding work in building an organization that is able to apply the same core skills to a different product. We simply have added to the hedge fund process a portfolio of shorted stocks in order to mitigate the risk that's associated with investing in the stock market. Additionally, we control risk by a tighter use of price stops to help avoid large losses in any one holding. We let our "bottom-up" approach to longs and shorts dynamically dictate our net exposure to the market."

In 2013, about 60 per cent of Formula Growth's assets under management were in its long/short hedge funds. "The customers are voting with their feet these days and seem to prefer the relative safety of our hedge funds," notes Kelly. "Interestingly, you don't really make a lot of money shorting, but a properly constructed short book helps control downside risk. You control the shorts, and if the market decides to implode on you, your short book will mitigate the losses. Additionally, in our long/short philosophy, we use cash defensively. We don't disrespect cash to the same extent that we did in the original Formula Growth Fund, where the fund was virtually always 100 per cent invested."

The Formula Growth Hedge Fund (FGHF) was launched on 1 December 2002 after several years of study, taking in new investors with a similar profile to those in the original Formula Growth: wealthy individuals, generally local, looking for something a little less volatile. "It was successful right away," says John Liddy. "We started with $2 million, basically all insiders, and a couple of outside investors. The offering memorandum was available only to net high-worth individuals, and it has grown steadily." Since its launch, it has compounded at over 20 per cent per year, notwithstanding the tough decade for US stocks.

According to Globe Funds, FGHF has already emerged as the number one alternative fund in Canada. "It is hard to achieve a ten-year record in the hedge fund space, never mind one with this kind of performance," says Kelly proudly. "There are thousands of hedge funds in the United States, but few survive for ten years."

HFR Group, a Chicago hedge fund consultant, has ranked FGHF as number twelve out of just 450 hedge funds that have a ten-year record. Randy Kelly is hopeful that FGHF is well on its way to achieving the type of fifty-year record that the original Formula Growth Fund has experienced.

In 2009, Formula Growth launched another hedge fund – Formula Growth Global Opportunities Fund (GOF) – which includes global stocks, with a focus on Asia. It currently has about $25 million in assets. This is a "back-to-the-future" move, reminiscent of the early days of Formula when Dobson met with great success by going off to Europe and Japan to find growth stocks. The Global Opportunities Fund is especially bullish on Greater China, which it describes as a region representing "the world's largest growth opportunity in the coming decades." In fact, in early 2013, nearly 100 per cent of the Fund's assets were invested there. In keeping with its investment approach of having a strong on-the-ground research presence and trusted information network, Formula Growth is pulling on the resources of Hong Kong-based Phoenix Investments, run by James Soutar, the son of Ian Soutar. James Soutar briefly worked for Formula Growth and has become a stellar investment manager in his own right.

CHAPTER 10

A Foe of Excessive Government

*John always felt that people were not educated at an
early enough stage about the benefits of wealth creation.*

— RANDY KELLY

As a passionate stock market investor, John Dobson never made any
excuses for his defence of the capitalist system as the best way of
organizing a nation's economy. He understood the role of government in providing social services, particularly for the less fortunate,
in building roads and schools, and providing society with the level
of security it needs. But when it comes to business, Dobson, like his
father before him, believed strongly that government can be most
effective when it steps aside and allows entrepreneurs and investors
the fullest opportunity to create wealth, jobs, and the economic
development that any society needs. For those reasons, he railed
throughout his life against excess taxation and over-regulation.

"I've always believed that the cost, mental frustration, and waste
of time caused by unproductive regulatory and government intrusion
stifle the entrepreneur and must be challenged," said Dobson.

∞ CAPITAL GAINS TAXES ∞

For over forty years, Dobson was a fervent opponent of capital
gains taxes, arguing with unrelenting passion that these levies hurt
investments and are detrimental to society as a whole. In 2000, he
presented a brief to the Standing Committee on Banking, Trade, and
Commerce and enjoyed a victory the following year when the government partially reduced Canadian capital gains taxes.

The Canadian government first introduced a tax on capital gains in 1972, declaring that it needed the revenues to finance the country's expanding social safety net and that the tax would assure a more equitable taxation system. Between 1972 and 1988, the inclusion rate (the amount of capital gains subject to taxation) stood at 50 per cent. Then, in 1988, it was raised to 67 per cent. Two years later, it rose again to 75 per cent. Under sharp criticism from the business community, the government re-established a lower rate of 67 per cent and then reset it again to 50 per cent, where it remains today. In other words, if you have a capital gain of $1,000, half of that sum is taxable. Individuals in the top tax bracket are taxed at approximately 43 per cent, so the tax on a capital gain of $1,000 now equals about $215.

That was still much too high for John Dobson. In fact, he wanted zero capital gains. "A high rate of capital gains tax is bad for all Canadians, not just the privileged few," he argued. "As investors, we are interested in wealth creation. That appears to be a bad term in Canada, so bad that it is neither used nor discussed. But I think that everyone accepts that the creation of jobs in the private sector requires someone to have capital. A high capital gains tax seriously eliminates opportunity and significantly contributes to the brain drain."

Dobson noted that what he terms "negative capital policies" can seriously harm the power of compounding interest, which he described as one of the "great wonders of the world." He loved to remind people that $1,000 compounded at 20 per cent for forty years untaxed becomes $1.5 million. However, $1,000 compounded at 20 per cent for forty years with an annual capital gains tax of 40 per cent becomes just $93,000. "Over forty years, the government receives, if taxed annually, $22,000. If the government only collected the tax at the end, it would have $600,000. What has happened here is that an individual ends up with $93,000 instead of $1.5 million of wealth creation, and the government gets $22,000. It is not a very good deal for anyone."

Insidiously, during periods of high inflation (generally caused by bad government policy), much of the return on an investment merely represents inflation, Dobson said. "In that instance, a capital gains tax simply represents a tax on inflation, or nominal return at best. There is no regard for real return, and that's wrong."

Moreover, because of capital gains tax, many people hesitate to make changes to their investment portfolios, leading to unnecessary losses when securities decline. "This locked-in factor is enormous and experienced by many portfolio owners and managers. There is a big economic loss from staying invested in lower investments and not switching to newer, faster-growing companies."

Some investors are also loath to invest money in Canada, choosing to go offshore instead, Dobson noted. "The biggest negative of all is the loss from entrepreneurs who never get started because of the effects of high capital gains tax. First, for those who choose to remain in Canada, there are not enough "angels" to finance startups because of the lack of wealth creation. Second, Canada loses when Canadians set up in the United States rather than in Canada because of the perceived uncompetitive climate caused by capital gains tax. That correlates directly with job creation."

Dobson argued that the revenue the federal government receives from capital gains taxes is not very significant due to cost and regulations. "The cost for collection and policing must be subtracted from the revenue. Because the capital gains tax is applied over a long time period, it is very complicated to keep score."

In his appearance before the Senate Committee on Banking, Trade, and Commerce chaired by Senator Leo Kolber in 2000, Dobson and Ian Soutar summed up their opposition to the capital gains tax as follows: "Canadians' well-being has been substantially lessened by the high capital gains tax that has been imposed by our government. First, the tax significantly reduces the wealth creation process. Second, the lock-in effect of the capital gains tax has badly affected returns by keeping Canadians from switching into higher-returning assets. Third, this high tax has either prevented our most talented entrepreneurial business people from getting started in Canada because of a lack of angel financing, or has driven them from the country. A reduced capital gains tax will not just help the rich. It will materially help all Canadians to enjoy a higher standard of living by creating the wealth that is needed to provide our citizens with better education, health care, or whatever else we choose collectively to spend it on."

∞ NEED FOR INVESTMENT EDUCATION ∞

Dobson regretted that the investment process itself is commonly perceived as being only for the rich. "I strongly believe that this is a very unfortunate perception caused by a lack of understanding of the process. Once you understand the wonderful power of compounding over long periods of time, you realize that the nation is losing enormously by not letting the egg grow to a great size."

Part of the problem is the fact that people are not educated at an early stage about the benefits of wealth creation. "There is a perception generally that, if people get rich, they are getting rich by some shady activity, whatever it may be. I also think there is a mentality in this country of envy – if the government does not do it for us, it is not right – and a mentality of dependence, where people would rather have the government do things for them than do them themselves. However, it is unfortunate that we do not have a more positive attitude about this issue. We seem to pride ourselves on writing articles in newspapers about people's salaries, about how much money they are making, and about their stock options. It is a very negative spin that we seem to put on it collectively, rather than putting a positive spin on it and saying 'Is it not wonderful that someone is getting rich because, if he or she gets rich, it will benefit all of us.'"

Dobson pointed his finger at schools and colleges where entrepreneurship is not often taught. "The economists – my dear friends – are giving a tremendously misleading statement about facts of life to our students in the schools. They say that, in economic-growth theory, innovation and technology are not part of it. We at Formula Growth have been investing for over fifty years in companies that are growing. Here is what is going on in the practical world."

The principal argument for a capital gains tax has traditionally been fairness and equity. But in Dobson's view, it has to do with an increased size of the pie. "If you talk to the taxi drivers in Montreal, they want business to boom. They want to see some more fat cats. There are not enough of them around. If you talk to the beggars and the various people in the street, for them to get off welfare, they need for someone to make the pie bigger, particularly in the private sector."

Dobson believed the best way to help society's disadvantaged is to make the safety net better and bigger, and the only way we can do that is to increase the size of the economy. "What are we going to do to increase the pie? We have to create some more productivity and wealth, and to do that, we have to have some capital."

In Dobson's ideal society, there would be much less government and an incentive system for the private sector to play a bigger role. "This issue about fairness gets in the way of making the economic pie larger for everyone," he said. "I believe that we'd all be better off if Canadians understood the process of wealth creation and the benefits they would derive from it. Let's face it, in the world, all is not fair."

In his presentation to the Senate Committee, Dobson listed Canada's chief attributes: a very small population, lots of fresh air and water, a low crime rate, and a population that is generally sympathetic to looking after the poor. "There are many wonderful things about Canada that have kept us all here, not just money. We have well-educated people and a great labour force. Many people here speak more than one language. We have all kinds of advantages. This is a very attractive place. However, in my opinion, where we are really uncompetitive is on this issue of capital gains tax. Yes, some of the money will go out, but more of it will be invested here. In general, I am very certain that we will be better off as a result of a lower capital gains tax rate."

⤜ BATTLES OVER SECURITIES REGULATIONS ⤛

Dobson believed that he probably could not have started Formula Growth Fund in the twenty-first century because of the capital gains tax and increased regulation. "I came out of industry. I had not been in the business. The Quebec Securities Commission would have thought that I probably would not be very suitable to run a fund."

In fact, over-zealous securities regulation and government red tape have long been sources of frustration to Dobson. From Formula Growth's earliest days, he was engaged in a tug-of-war with Quebec securities regulators over whether Formula Growth should be subject to the same oversight as mutual funds several times its size with a wide distribution to the public.

From the outset, Formula Growth saw itself as an "investment club," perhaps larger than most, but definitely not as a "mutual fund." It had no salesmen, and it paid no commissions to anyone for the sale of units. It was like a club because nobody could simply walk off the street and buy units. "In fact, we knew every client who invested in the fund," says Randy Kelly. "We were ahead of our time in this respect. Today, financial institutions and others are 'getting to know their clients,' preparing personal profiles, and so on. At the same time, we were not interested in growing the unit count or getting big."

The Fund's success quickly attracted the attention of the Quebec Securities Commission (QSC) – since 2004 known as the Autorité des marchés financiers (AMF) – which argued that it was essentially a mutual fund and, as such, should be required to issue a prospectus that pointed out the risks to investors. "The QSC was very alarmed when we had a fair chunk of the Fund in Japan," recalls Walter Cottingham, who helped to establish Formula Growth in 1960. "In those times, Japan could impose currency controls, and the Commission wanted us to put in our prospectus, in big print, that there is a danger that you could not get your money out of Japan. I remember hashing that out with the QSC."

The give-and-take with the QSC went on for years, with Formula Growth eventually being forced to acquiesce and issue a prospectus. But it was not without a fight. On 6 September 1963, the three managers – Dobson, Walter Cottingham, and John Rook – wrote to QSC Commissioner J.B. Doran, arguing that Formula Growth shouldn't be forced to issue a prospectus.

"After speaking with executives of several of the large funds in Montreal, they said the common opinion was that Formula Growth was an investment syndicate rather than a mutual fund," they wrote. "It had no sales load or salesmen. It was far below the $10 million in assets generally accepted as being a minimum for an economic business operation. Further, without the use of salesmen and a sales commission, it was felt that we would never attain this figure." (Formula Growth and its sister institutional fund attained assets of over $1 billion Canadian at their peak in 2000). "The fact that the Formula Growth Fund units are not transferable gives the management absolute discretion as to what type of person will be permitted to become a member of the Fund."

The Fund managers also balked at a QSC concern that some investors could be hurt by Formula Growth's plans to borrow money to invest, and by its intention to levy a "performance fee" of a half of 1 per cent per year (up to a maximum of $50,000) if the Fund performed 5 per cent better than the Dow Jones Industrial Average during any calendar year.

"We feel that in the draft prospectus, we have bent over backwards to spell out our method of operation and have provided 'full disclosure.' Perhaps we should put the information about leverage in capital letters or write a new leverage section. We feel it is not fair to all our unit holders to be put in a position where collectively they are unable to take advantage of prudent operations just because some individuals might get hurt. The big thing is to make sure that all unit holders understand what they are buying."

Because 20 per cent of the Fund belonged to the managers and their families, and much of the rest belonged to their friends and associates, with unit holders investing an average $9,000 apiece, Dobson, Walter Cottingham, and John Rook argued that they should be trusted to manage other people's money as if it were their own. "We would not wish to be put in a position where we ask people to invest with us but are not able to do for them what we do for ourselves. People can invest dollar for dollar on the same basis as our own money. Theoretically, if the Fund is denied the intelligent investment practice of a conservative degree of leverage, we should take our own money out of the pool and invest it individually."

"As far as we are concerned," the trio concluded, "we are members of a private syndicate, albeit a large one in numbers (although I am sure that there are much larger private syndicates in dollar amount), who have banded together to increase our access to information and influence in obtaining favourable participations in attractive new issues throughout the world."

Despite their protests, Formula Growth was ordered in the mid-1960s to file a prospectus, albeit a thin one, which it continued to do for several years until reaching a compromise with the QSC in the 1970s. It came to that agreement with the help of Stuart ("Kip") Cobbett, who was Formula Growth's secretary and lawyer. "I was successful in negotiating a specific arrangement with the QSC that permitted Formula Growth to operate without filing a prospectus," says Cobbett, today a lawyer at Stikeman Elliott and chair of McGill's board of governors. "It was a not a private investment club in the sense that it had members of the public as unit holders. But the QSC recognized that it was a very limited universe of people that were investing in Formula Growth, and they were prepared to treat it on a different basis than a normal mutual fund."

Nevertheless, the damage had already been done. Even though it stopped issuing prospectuses, Formula Growth was subject to QSC rules and regulations for years to come. René Catafago, the Fund's long-time CFO, says, "When we would make presentations to the QSC, we'd say we were a private fund, that we're not subject to all those rules and regulations of a particular fund. But they'd say we were because we had a prospectus thirty years ago. Even though we never used one, once you've issued a prospectus, you're bound to have the same rules·and regulations. We couldn't get (around) those specific regulations."

The legacy of the QSC's requirement that Formula Growth issue a prospectus resulted in more paperwork, staff, and expense for over forty years. "We used to manage a lot of money, with very little staff because the regulations were not the same in those days," says René Catafago. "We used to do business on a handshake. If somebody wanted to come into the fund, there wasn't even a subscription agreement. We were managing over $1 billion dollars in 2000, and we had less than ten people on staff. Now we manage a little over half that, and we have sixteen people on the payroll, while having to pay a small fortune to outside consultants, lawyers, accountants and administrators! There are a lot of people in administration because there's so much red tape." Formula Growth used to pay the QSC about $1,800 a year in fees. With the increased involvement of lawyers, it now spends close to $500,000 a year in various administrative expenses.

René Catafago used to get a lot of requests for administrative information about Formula Growth from brokerage firms, investment banks, and other interested parties and admits that he often would simply ignore them, figuring that if they really needed a written response, they would ask a second time. "And it worked! A hallmark of Formula Growth is that our word or our handshake is our bond," he says. "We do not need the extra administrative burden of writing everything down, especially with the expensive help of lawyers. When we say we are going to do something, we do it."

Employees of Formula Growth are also very large owners of its products, and this ensures the firm's behaviour will always be beyond reproach, Catafago adds. "We have never had a complaint because, importantly, we have never done anything incorrect. In our fifty-year history, we have never been sanctioned by a regulatory authority or had any compliance issues. There has never been a number out of place. We have been able to focus on just one thing, and it is the wealth of our clients. And we have done a damn good job of it, because a lot of people have made a lot of money with us."

Dobson believed that over-regulation was wasteful and misguided, not to mention counterproductive. "What I think the regulators are doing wrong is that they're taking money raised from fees and levies and building nice offices and teams of sleuths to investigate honest companies. What they should be doing instead is using that money to educate the public, beginning at a young age, on how to invest – and especially on what not to do when they invest. I don't see anything, on billboards or on TV, telling you how to invest wisely and avoid being cheated. As a result, we still have crooks like Bernie Madoff who take advantage of people and hurt public confidence in investing. It's not right."

CHAPTER 11

Supporting Entrepreneurship and the Free Enterprise System

> *[My father] showed me how important it is to use all the means at one's disposal to create opportunities for others and contribute to a better society.*

— JOHN DOBSON

John Dobson has been described as "the venture capitalist of entrepreneurship education" in Canada – someone willing to buck tradition, take calculated risks, and change the game. And for good reason. Through his John Dobson Foundation, he funded dozens of initiatives across the country – from university centres offering courses in entrepreneurship and outreach programs in the community to think-tanks promoting free markets and low taxation. His philanthropic support and willingness to try new approaches have helped to change the way entrepreneurship is taught and promoted, and have spawned generations of new entrepreneurs.

"John Dobson was a visionary and outstanding leader for entrepreneurship in Canada and across the world," says Teresa Menzies, a professor of entrepreneurship and family business at Brock University's Faculty of Business. Menzies published a series of national reports on Entrepreneurship Education and Entrepreneurship Centres in Canada funded by the John Dobson Foundation. "His ideas and support ignited and fuelled a pragmatic approach to universities and entrepreneurship development." In the words of Senator Kelvin Ogilvie, former president and vice-chancellor of Acadia University in Wolfville, Nova Scotia, where he led the development and implementation of the acclaimed Acadia Advantage Program, "John Dobson was almost unique in the way he understood the need to instill entrepreneurship in young people, particularly at the college and university level, by giving them the tools and stressing that it doesn't have to be related to a business degree. Many of John's proteges have become very successful entrepreneurs."

Dobson said the creation of his Foundation was a natural outgrowth of a lifelong passion for investing in promising and entrepreneurial companies and a fitting way to give back to the community. "From a very young age, my father gave me a deep respect for free enterprise and self-reliance. At the same time, he showed me how important it was to use all the means at one's disposal to create opportunities for others and contribute to a better society."

For Dobson, the formula was simple: a more entrepreneurial country means more jobs and more wealth for everyone. He was driven by a few simple goals: to increase opportunities for creating entrepreneurs, leading to more jobs; to get more people to create enterprises; and to better understand the process of enterprise creation. Dobson's main goal was to give people an opportunity, a chance to reach their full potential. If he saw people with talent, he tried to give them an opportunity to fulfill their dreams. He was constantly on the lookout for somebody who was an innovator and wanted to do something different.

And Dobson believed that universities have a role to play in fostering entrepreneurship. "For years, John was ahead of his time because, in the early days, there was not a significant academic body of knowledge supporting that word 'entrepreneurship' in universities," says Senator Ogilvie. "It was considered something for others to do. Universities did not really embrace it until recent years. Now, it's part of the academic curriculum in virtually every school, and it has gained a lot of legitimacy."

∞ CREATING THE FOUNDATION ∞

Dobson decided to take a more formal approach to educating the public about the free enterprise system and entrepreneurial activities in Canada by establishing the John Dobson Foundation. Founded 1986, the Foundation was initially endowed with a donation of $1.8 million from Dobson's personal investment portfolio, much of it generated by a highly successful investment in Jackson National Life, a US insurance company. Joining Dobson as the Foundation's first directors were David Laidley, Ian Soutar, and Jacques Tétrault.

The Foundation strives to stimulate the formation and growth of small companies by promoting tax incentives, less bureaucratic interference, and a wider understanding by the Canadian public of the positive impact that new companies have on job creation. The basic mission of the Foundation is to educate the public about entrepreneurial activities and to make Canada a dynamic and entrepreneurial country. Over the years, its emphasis has evolved more toward promoting entrepreneurship, with a secondary focus on supporting think-tanks that encourage free-market thinking, and a third mandate to promote investment education.

The Foundation has undoubtedly had its greatest impact in its support of entrepreneurship centres in universities across the country. "We have tried to foster an educational environment that will set the stage for creating productive jobs for Canadians," said Dobson. "One of the major activities within this mission is to encourage educational institutions to expose their students to the benefits and opportunities of pursuing entrepreneurial activities. Historically, over 90 per cent of new jobs come from small companies."

To date, the John Dobson Foundation has assisted in supporting entrepreneurship programs in more than twenty universities and colleges: Acadia, Bishop's, Cape Breton, Dalhousie, McMaster, Mount Royal, Mount St Vincent, Nova Scotia Community College, Ryerson, St Mary's, St Francis Xavier, Simon Fraser, University of Toronto, University of British Columbia, University of New Brunswick,

University of Prince Edward Island, Wilfrid Laurier, Windsor, McGill, Concordia, Sainte Anne, Brock, Mount Allison, Waterloo, and Memorial. It also sponsors several entrepreneurial-related competitions, including the Student Entrepreneur National Competition and a competition at Loyola High School in Montreal.

Many of these programs were assessed and evaluated for the purposes of Foundation support by the late Norm Keesal, a former professor at McGill's Management Institute and a trusted confidant of Dobson's. "After I retired, John asked me to help the John Dobson Foundation set up entrepreneur institutes similar to the one at McGill in other institutions across Canada," said Keesal, who attended Harvard Business School at the same time as Dobson did. "Other universities had started to approach him, and he wasn't sure exactly where to go. I spent much time in the Maritimes visiting the schools that were asking for help and coming back and telling John where I thought he ought to put his money."

Keesal described Dobson as a man who always put his money where his mouth was. "He was one of the most practical and vigorous supporters of Canadian growth by backing an incredible range of programs and activities designed to help our bright, young people develop as the builders of our country by building companies and programs of their own."

Norm Keesal and Dobson had crossed paths for decades. After graduating from Harvard, Keesal went to work for two years with investment counselling firm Stein Roe & Farnham in his hometown of Chicago. "We had some very good clients, including two former US presidents. It was a big operation. I thought I was going to pass out when I realized how much money I had been responsible for. Hundreds of millions! But I would do research and came to the conclusion – probably like John did – that sitting around watching other people do things was no good for me."

In 1954, a former classmate asked Keesal to partner in a small company he had started in Montreal. Keesal gave his notice and drove up to Canada. He left that venture to help another friend run

Cartier Chemicals, a company specializing in industrial and sanitation chemicals. Soon he started teaching part-time at the Executive Development Course being run by Bill Turner. "At the same time, John started to teach there, and we became much closer friends. We'd have dinner every time we'd both be teaching our classes."

Working as a consultant to the John Dobson Foundation, Norm Keesal acted as a source of information about how things are done, evaluating what the schools are doing with their grants and guiding them. "Our focus is first and foremost on student involvement. We want to get them involved and interested in what's going on. We want to help get things started. We don't want long-term commitments. The initial push is always the hardest, but that's where we come in. One thing universities don't do very well is get students ready for the real world, so we've been pushing that pretty hard."

The Foundation has continually emphasized the need to get faculties, outside of business schools, involved in entrepreneurship education. "We have found that the majority of successful new ideas and innovations come from entrepreneurs who attended non-business school faculties," said Dobson. It turns out that business students are not natural risk takers. In fact, statistics show that it is non-business students who are most likely to go into business for themselves. "Simon Fraser was one university that liked the idea of getting courses and programs of entrepreneurship into the other faculties," said Keesal. "They bought in. We gave them some money to start, and a smaller amount for the next two years to help them get it going. Now they've got three courses with fifty students in each. There are three other faculties that are standing by to get an entrepreneurship course."

McGill is another example. Some years ago, it started offering an entrepreneurship course for engineering students, which has evolved into a minor in entrepreneurship. University of British Columbia (UBC) also has a program that mixes business and engineering students, notes Keesal. "Engineers have ideas and don't know what to do with them. Business students have no ideas, but would know what to do with them!" The Foundation supports an MBA program for engineers at McMaster, as well as one at the University of Waterloo, that gets engineers involved with starting their own businesses.

Nevertheless, Teresa Menzies says that most Canadian universities still have a long way to go in terms of offering entrepreneurship courses to non-business students. A census she prepared in 2009 showed that only 2.4 per cent of Canadian university students took an entrepreneurship course in the 2008–09 academic year. "I know that John was disappointed, as am I, in our slow progress toward getting entrepreneurship as a core course for every student at every university in Canada. This should be the norm. It is fast becoming the norm in some countries. But Canada, which used to be in the forefront of entrepreneurship education, looks like it could be left behind. What do we do? We are up against prejudice, tradition, politics, turf wars, and so on. That said, much of the success achieved to date is due in large part to John Dobson. He was the charismatic leader who supported and challenged the Canadian entrepreneurship group."

The John Dobson Foundation has also broadened its reach beyond academia. "The University of New Brunswick ran a program that the Foundation helped start, which said to the community, 'If you have an idea for a new business but need help, come to us,'" said Norm Keesal. "They accepted five applicants for the first year and found a couple of students to co-ordinate the program. If the company needed to have some market research done, they'd assign a group of students to do the research. The finance group came up with the financing idea, and the accounting students set up the books. One business started there now has 300 employees. What John Dobson did was phenomenal. He was unbelievable. In the States, there's the Kaufman Foundation that has been doing this for a very long time. But in Canada, it's the John Dobson Foundation."

The Foundation also promotes mentoring and encourages college students to get involved in their communities and members of the business community to collaborate with local colleges. "Our most recent new successes have come from our projects involving pre-college students," noted Dobson. "For mentoring, the Foundation looks to support and promote passionate individuals who, in many cases, have practical business experience. Students respond to, get motivated by, and learn most from people who have created and run businesses."

Throughout his life, Dobson had been reluctant to give large endowments to universities since he was skeptical that money donated this way would be well invested or wisely spent. "John, in a sense, viewed universities as quasi-governmental organizations and was suspicious of bureaucracy, as we well know," explained Randy Kelly. "That's why he never funded a university chair, preferring instead to target money for specific programs, which can be carefully monitored. He also was not impressed with the rather paltry rates of return earned by many university endowment funds and felt it was better for him to earn a much higher return and donate the proceeds accordingly."

Dobson also believed new activities should be funded by his foundation for only a limited number of years. "Our view is that if they are successful, projects will be self-sustaining or they will attract others to support them," he explained. "As a result, the Foundation can exit and find new entrepreneurial projects that need funding. We've never wanted to create a dependency." Dobson ran the Foundation to achieve maximum impact while keeping costs low. There is no full-time administrator, and Formula Growth's regular staffers volunteer their time to provide all the support, thus assuring that funds are available for projects rather than for administration.

The Foundation was financed personally by Dobson from a portfolio that he invested himself. Rather than selling the stock and be subject to capital gains tax, he donated shares that had risen substantially in value to the Foundation. While there have also been small donations made by outsiders, most of the funds have come from Dobson. The Foundation distributes as much as $2 million per year, for a total of more than $26 million since 1992, and at the current rate of spending, it has sufficient funds to continue its work indefinitely.

☾ THE DOBSON CENTRE ☽
FOR ENTREPRENEURIAL STUDIES

One of the first initiatives undertaken by the John Dobson Foundation, and which remains a centrepiece today, is the Dobson Centre for Entrepreneurial Studies at McGill University, established in 1989. However, finding a director took some time, in part because of Dobson's insistence that the Centre be led by someone with practical experience.

When a suitable candidate could not be found, Dobson suggested Montreal businessman Peter Johnson (whom Dobson had met through David Laidley), an old friend and a former chairman of Deloitte Touche. Johnson had no academic background, but he was a long-time entrepreneur who had recently sold his two companies – equipment rental firm Perco Ltd., and Aqua d'Or, a water treatment concern. Johnson was about to buy another company when Laidley, who had provided Johnson with professional services over the years, approached him about leading the McGill project. Dobson and Johnson immediately clicked, and Dobson decided he had found his man.

"My interview with the dean of the management faculty was about thirty seconds long since John Dobson had recommended me," Johnson recalls. "John gave McGill about $1.4 million for the Centre, and the Zeller Family Foundation, which I chaired, gave another million dollars. The mandate was to teach entrepreneurship and start the Centre." (The John Dobson Foundation's total contribution to McGill would grow to a total of $3.5 million over the years.) Dobson's judgment proved right on the mark. Despite Johnson's lack of university experience, he was named by students as best teacher in the management faculty at the end of his first year. Johnson has no regrets about taking on the job. "David Laidley asked if I would take two years out of my life to work at McGill, and I ended up spending sixteen years there," Johnson says.

When the Dobson Centre for Entrepreneurial Studies was set up, there were only two other universities in Canada that did entrepreneurship mentoring: Acadia and Brock. "John basically funded the three of us [McGill, Acadia, Brock] right off the bat," according to Johnson. "Now there are twenty-two universities with programs like this."

David Lank joined three years later. "The emphasis was on experience rather than theory. The Centre became the finest centre for entrepreneurial studies in North America thanks to its courses, distinguished professors, and outstanding lecturers from across McGill. It was also innovative by combining arts, music, and philosophy with entrepreneurship."

Lank, who is now director emeritus of the Dobson Centre, first met Dobson forty years ago when Lank's father was chairman of DuPont Canada. Dobson's promotion of entrepreneurship was particularly important in Montreal at a time when it was losing its attraction as a head-office city and business graduates could no longer depend on finding good corporate jobs locally. "John was very enthusiastic and a risk taker, a really powerful, positive influence," says Lank. "He trumpeted the importance of SMEs [small- and medium-sized enterprises] and entrepreneurship in a city where universities are trying to satisfy a head office market that's no longer there. He wanted to introduce concepts of entrepreneurship at the high-school level. He believed entrepreneurship is really important."

David Lank, a founder of Helix Investments, a large venture-capital firm, worked for eleven years at the Dobson Centre for Entrepreneurial Studies and also sat on the board of advisors of the John Dobson Foundation. "I pushed for John Dobson to become a brand, to do things under his name. He made a huge contribution, and we're all indebted to him."

The Dobson Centre for Entrepreneurial Studies has become the symbol of what can happen in a research-oriented institution when practical people are given the support and encouragement of a practicing visionary. Thousands of students have been taught, inspired, and polished through their interaction with real people with real experience and through sharing the accumulated wisdom of the business world and of their professors. The Centre currently has five faculty members who offer a variety of courses ranging from governance to finance. It runs an annual McGill Dobson Cup competition, with a top prize of $40,000, welcomes guest speakers, and has an outreach program for the community.

Angela Burlton has been involved with the Centre since the late 1990s. Her father-in-law, Roger DeSerres, was an investor and early board member of Formula Growth. Burlton herself first met Dobson in the late 1970s and was taken with him from the start. "He was very engaged and had a real heart of gold," says Burlton. After obtaining her CA, Burlton joined McGill's management faculty in 1999 and took over leadership of the Centre from Peter Johnson. "Our goal is to help people become more familiar with what it is to be entrepreneurial," she says.

Burlton notes that the number of students who want to launch their own companies right after university has grown in recent years. "Because of a shift to cheaper markets, people have to be more ingenious about how they earn a living." Her classes attract different kinds of students. "There are the born entrepreneurs. You could drop them in the middle of Shanghai and, within two weeks, they'll have created a business. Then there are the entrepreneurs who need a little help to get started. And the third type is those who will always work for employers, but will bring an entrepreneurial edge to their work."

All told, the John Dobson Foundation has helped more than sixty organizations involved in entrepreneurship in Canada. "Sometimes John wouldn't give money to certain people for various reasons, but he made decisions quickly," says Johnson. "He had an unbelievable passion of more, more, more! He was always willing to take a chance and try things."

In Peter Johnson's view, Dobson drove a model to be emulated by the rest of the world. "It's all about changing the job mix to more service-oriented fields and to have more entrepreneurial companies. Manufacturing will keep going to China and India, which have two billion people and much lower labour costs. We need to educate people to change the job mix with more services. The Quebec and Ontario governments, to their credit, have centres across the provinces that provide mentoring and help for people to start their own businesses. The Business Development Bank of Canada has done an extraordinary job over many years, and John Dobson also funded various projects through them."

Johnson notes that when he and Dobson used to go to entrepreneurship conferences across the country, the twenty-two universities that the Foundation funded were the kingpins. "John Dobson was at the forefront of this in Canada. No one else has done work like this. Sometimes he'd call his friends from across the country and share in the making of documentaries of successful entrepreneurs, which are shown in class."

The Dobson Centre for Entrepreneurial Studies is also involved in outreach in the broader Montreal community, with students mentoring an average of 300 to 400 people at a time to help them start businesses. Building on this, the John Dobson Foundation helped to launch a centre called YES (Youth Employment Services), a non-profit organization that provides English-language support services to help young Quebecers find jobs and start businesses. YES also offers advice to young people starting businesses with the help of 125 mentors, most of them retirees, and holds an annual entrepreneurship conference that often showcases business owners who started their enterprises at a young age.

☜ GIVING STUDENTS THE ADVANTAGE ☞

The John Dobson Foundation was instrumental in turning Nova Scotia's Acadia University into a showcase for entrepreneurial education in Canada. It all began when long-time entrepreneurial educator Chris Pelham met John Dobson in 1997 through Acadia fundraiser Harvey Gilmour. "Harvey had asked John for financial support to computerize Acadia's campus," recalls Pelham. "John said no but offered to support anything in entrepreneurship, so Harvey asked me for ideas."

The result was key financial support for the Acadia Centre for Small Business and Entrepreneurship (now called the Acadia Centre for Social and Business Entrepreneurship, or ACSBE), a non-profit organization affiliated with the university that provides a range of leading-edge entrepreneurial programming. The Centre innovated by reaching out to students in all disciplines and by assisting students with the development of the skills and attitudes necessary to think and act entrepreneurially. The overall objective is to have students pursue personal success, says Pelham, who became the Centre's second executive director, in 1991.

Pelham was surprised to discover that business students at Acadia were among the least likely to embark on a small business career. Only divinity students showed less interest. "Business students were not interested in becoming entrepreneurs. Music, science, and kinesiology students had a higher interest," says Pelham.

With that in mind, Pelham wanted to find a way to expand the concept of entrepreneurship across the university and to dispel misconceptions that the university was attempting to teach students how to use business to take advantage of others. "We argued that it's more complicated than that; we're teaching a life skill." Pelham made a proposal to Dobson: entrepreneurship is not only about business. It's also about developing students' capacity to take risks, to make decisions, and to take some action. "For example, in music, you don't just learn theory; you learn how to play an instrument and how to take it apart, tune it, and make it better. It's the same with entrepreneurship."

Chris Pelham arrived at Formula Growth's offices with Harvey Gilmour, an Acadia student, and a PowerPoint presentation. "I left it up to Harvey to negotiate. Harvey and John were trying to figure out a dollar figure, and it wasn't going anywhere. Then the student put her hand up. Everybody thought she had a solution to the impasse.

But all she did was ask if somebody would pass the cookies. That broke the ice! We got $125,000 for three years and a promise to help raise more."

That marked the beginning of a fifteen-year relationship with Dobson. He supported a range of activities that Acadia has undertaken to show that entrepreneurship is not just for business people. "From day one, our mantra was 'Entrepreneurship is the development of a life skill,'" says Pelham, who was awarded the 2005 Life Achievement Award from the Canadian Council for Small Business and Entrepreneurship (CCSBE) for his contribution to the development of entrepreneurial education.

It was not smooth going, especially at first. "We got laughed at a lot in the beginning, even ridiculed," says Pelham. "We didn't always have successful ventures with John's money. We went back and said this is what we're trying to do, we're getting ridiculed ... and he continued to support us. He said this is the right way to develop the entrepreneurship culture. John even went back to his alma mater, Harvard, and said, 'Look, if you guys want to know how we're developing entrepreneurship at the university level, talk to Acadia.' Lots of places have adapted our approach. We are no longer laughed at. Entrepreneurship is now seen as a life skill."

Senator Kelvin Ogilvie, Acadia's former president, says ACSBE has been very successful in involving undergraduates in small businesses around the university. "It tried to trigger entrepreneurial instincts among students, to see what the challenges were. These students would help with the business's early business plans, websites, spreadsheets, etc. ACSBE is a separate entity, managed outside of any academic department, and its employees were not direct employees of the university."

In 1996, Ogilvie introduced the Acadia Advantage Program, making his university the first in Canada to be totally wired. Each student was provided with a laptop or desktop computer and an Internet connection to each desk. "At that time, students began to undertake more entrepreneurial activities. Software development in the music school, for example, was very successful. There was a natural pull to Acadia for entrepreneurship."

Ogilvie wanted to find a way to raise awareness about the program among other students to encourage them not to be afraid of developing a business. "We launched a competition across all faculties for entrepreneurship, which was supported by the John Dobson Foundation."

In 2008, Chris Pelham helped to organize a colloquium on entrepreneurial education and invited university and community college educators from across the country to Acadia to learn all about the good, the bad, and the ugly. "We thought it would be wonderful to have John make a presentation to sixty or seventy educational institutions. He agreed, to our surprise, but on one condition: that he would stay for an international conference on entrepreneurship being held a few days later. I was responsible for his agenda for four to five days, and we had a grand time. He was opinionated and assertive, but he was a pretty sensitive and fair guy as well. Acadia gave him an honorary doctorate, and I was asked to direct and give the citation, and I'm not an academic. He was taken by the fact Acadia would allow that."

Dobson did not want his name associated with initiatives at Acadia, but a Dobson lecture series was developed and incorporated into faculty programs. He also became involved in the Atlantic Institute for Market Studies, an independent, free-market-oriented think-tank based in Halifax, founded by economist Brian Lee Crowley. Dobson funded some of the Institute's special projects, including one conducted by Ogilvie that studied the feasibility of turning a Canadian public university into a private institution. "John was one of the truly unique and great Canadians of our time," says Ogilvie. "I greatly admired his dedication to our country, to building an entrepreneurial society, and his selfless support of bright young Canadians."

Dobson's influence was also felt in a big way at Wilfrid Laurier University in Waterloo. In the early 2000s, the university decided to create a centre for entrepreneurship and wanted to hire an entrepreneur to lead and direct it, as opposed to a pure academic. Scott Carson, dean of Laurier's School of Business and Economics at the time, had spoken with Dobson, who agreed to pay for the executive director's salary for three years. The director chosen was Steve Farlow, a lifelong entrepreneur who had just sold his company, Superior Safety, a distributor of health and safety products, to a publicly traded company in Houston.

"Back in those days, if John Dobson liked you and the program fit his general mission and purposes, then you were in," quips Farlow. "It took sixty seconds for him to make his decision." Farlow was appointed founding executive director of the Schlegel Centre for Entrepreneurship that operates within Laurier's School of Business and Economics. "John Dobson invested in creative initiatives that are outside the norm, outside the standard curriculum," he says. "He was always interested in very distinctive programs."

In addition to the Foundation's seed funding, which helped attract financial support from elsewhere, the John Dobson Foundation provided Farlow with lots of coaching, mentoring, and support. Dobson and Peter Johnson would also occasionally bring heads of entrepreneurship schools to Montreal to compare notes. "We'd report on our programs with a view of the challenges we were facing, and how we could all help each other," says Farlow. "That's a role the John Dobson Foundation played that was very helpful. He always would want to know how the projects would be sustainable. As a result, there are programs across the country that are now part of the culture of universities and colleges. This may not have happened had it not been for the early support of the John Dobson Foundation."

Many of these achievements were documented in the series of reference guides prepared by Teresa Menzies with funding from the Foundation. The most recent came out in 2009 and was entitled "Entrepreneurship & the Canadian Universities: Strategies and Best Practices." It features twenty-seven chapters, each written by a representative of a different school about its entrepreneurship program.

The next stage in the evolution of an entrepreneurship program at Wilfrid Laurier is to create opportunities for students to launch and build real enterprises within the academic curriculum. As such, students get course credits for creating businesses, with the John Dobson Foundation providing financial support to get the entrepreneurship programs going. Several schools now run "incubators" – at Laurier, it is called an accelerator centre – right within their schools.

The Laurier Entrepreneurship Accelerator Program brings together students from a number of faculties, including social sciences, arts, and music, along with alumni, mentors, and other partners, to create real businesses. "John Dobson was the first one in and allowed us to raise additional money," notes Steve Farlow. "When I make presentations to the Ontario government, other foundations, and entrepreneurs or companies, I always point to the John Dobson Foundation's early support as a clear indicator that brings legitimacy to the program. John loved this. In my pitches to him, I told him the plan and how we'd use his funds to raise additional funds. My dealings with John were tremendously high energy, cordial, professional, but to the point. He didn't suffer fools. When you saw him, you had to know exactly what you wanted to discuss, be succinct, and to the point."

Not all of the initiatives supported by the John Dobson Foundation have worked out. A significant disappointment was the "EntreNet," which was designed to host an online community of entrepreneurship educators across Canada. EntreNet was conceived around 2006, when online communities were just becoming mainstream. "After one of our big networking sessions, we decided to create an online platform to share course outlines and so on," says Farlow. "It was designed to be basically an online version of our meetings. It was a superb idea. But good ideas don't always work."

With about $300,000 in Foundation money, Steve Farlow, Peter Johnson, and others worked with a technology platform developed by CIGI (Centre for International Governance and Innovation) in Waterloo, Ontario, to create EntreNet. "The plan was to charge

$2,000 for a university to have access to it. We created a robust platform, but we were ahead of our time," says Farlow

The organizers soon found that professors were reluctant to share their course information, making it hard to generate content. At the same time, institutions resented paying the $2,000 sign-up fee. "All of a sudden, technology started to catch up, and people expected it to be free," says Farlow. "We did go after some sponsors to display logos. It was such hard work! An entrepreneurship community in the United States did the same thing subsequent to us but offered it for free and with a simpler technology platform. After two or three years, we closed EntreNet down, since it was not being adopted. Technology had caught up, and we could share this information for free. It brought a lot of people together, but, ultimately, it failed. But you have to take risks and chances."

Farlow says Dobson was respectful about the failure. "He discussed lessons learned and we moved on. There was no finger pointing or blame. We acknowledged our responsibilities in this project. It was not for lack of effort. It just didn't work. It shows that the John Dobson Foundation is willing to try things that others won't. Lots of programs worked, but this one didn't. We learned a ton from this project's failure."

∽ TARGETED SUPPORT ∾

Dobson's championing of entrepreneurship extended far beyond the university community, as reflected by his support for three organizations: Enactus Canada (a Toronto-based company formerly known as Advancing Canadian Entrepreneurship, or ACE, and prior to that, the Association of Collegiate Entrepreneurs), the Next 36 (based in Toronto), and the Montreal Economic Institute.

Ian Aitken, founder of Enactus Canada and a long-time champion of entrepreneurship, first crossed paths with Dobson while working as a summer student at Pembroke Management in Montreal in the mid-1980s. He later joined Pembroke and rose to become its president and CEO. At the time, Pembroke and Formula Growth worked closely together on investment prospecting. Aitken met Dobson again while attending the University of Western Ontario, where he was taking commerce and became heavily involved in entrepreneurial activities. "John was impressed with these activities and arranged for me to be on scholarship, so I was very grateful. I made a point of staying in touch with him and letting him know what I was working on."

While he was a student at Western, Aitken was a founding member and later president of an entrepreneurs' club, which went on to have over 800 members. In 1986, he also created the Canadian Association of University Student Entrepreneurs (C.A.U.S.E.), an umbrella group for entrepreneur clubs from across Canada, with the goal of exchanging best practices and encouraging the formation of new clubs. "I wanted other clubs to benefit from what we were doing and help create clubs in other universities."

Ian Aitken told Dobson about his initiative, and Dobson asked how much money he needed. "He wrote a cheque the same day. I was stunned. But this is typical of how John worked – he tried to back good people who do interesting things. He backed them early, and was often the first to do so." (Over twenty-five years later, Aitken continues to work closely with the John Dobson Foundation and has been a member of the board since 1999. Around 2006, he bought a house on Mountain Street in Montreal and invited Dobson over. It turned out that Dobson had lived in the house as a child. "He knew I had bought a house near where he lived, but they had renumbered all the houses so he didn't know it was the one until he walked in the front door.")

During 1987, C.A.U.S.E. changed its name to Canadian Association of Student Entrepreneurs (C.A.S.E.) so that college campuses could be included. A year later, it became the Association of Collegiate Entrepreneurs Canada and then Advancing Canadian Entrepreneurship (ACE). Today, known as Enactus Canada and chaired by Ian Aitken, it remains one of the driving forces for entrepreneurship in Canada. The John Dobson Foundation, Enactus

Canada's first donor, is its largest single donor today. "If John hadn't written that first cheque, this progress would never have happened," says Aitken. "Enactus became one of the projects he felt was a good example of what he wanted to do more of."

"The Foundation is very selective of the causes it wants to support because Dobson didn't want a hundred people asking for money," Aitken says. "That's why the Foundation keeps a relatively low profile." But Enactus Canada has long been a favourite. Dobson said the reason is clear. "We have supported Enactus for more than twenty years because it has delivered results in an efficient and effective manner. Of all the organizations we have supported, Enactus is the jewel in the crown."

Enactus president Nicole Almond says the organization has grown significantly over the past two decades, and the John Dobson Foundation has been instrumental in its development. "Each year, we grow not just in numbers, but in terms of the impact we have on youth and the impact they have on their communities. We are transforming lives and building a better Canada."

"We're big believers in the potential of youth to make a difference, and John Dobson believed in this, too," says Almond. "Across Canada, our student teams are taking an entrepreneurial approach to solving local community issues. We never settle for the status quo. We pursue targets that are well beyond our means, and we generally hit them. Our community empowerment projects and business ventures would not be possible without the support of entrepreneurial champions like John Dobson, who recognize us as very hungry entrepreneurs who are constantly reaching for new levels of success, while maintaining a progressive value system."

Many famous young Canadian entrepreneurs have belonged to Enactus Canada, including Brian Scudamore, CEO and founder of 1-800-GOT-JUNK, who credits the organization with giving him a forum to dream, share, and discuss ideas.

Under the leadership of Ian Aitken, Enactus Canada started as a collection of entrepreneurship clubs in various universities. "We were simply looking for a national platform to talk to one another," says Nicole Almond. "At first, the majority of our activities revolved around conferences. We would bring together university students to hear from entrepreneurs and to talk about what it means to be an entrepreneur. But after more than twenty-five years, we are now a truly national movement with thousands of students engaged annually at over sixty universities and colleges, from St John's, Newfoundland, to Victoria, British Columbia.

Enactus students start and operate businesses and develop projects that go out into the community. They identify a need and fill it. For example, at Memorial University of Newfoundland, the Enactus team is running an entrepreneurship transition program for military personnel in partnership with the Department of National Defence. It is known as Based in Business. The program identifies military personnel who are in transition, returning to civilian life, and brings them to St John's for a week-long intensive "boot camp," with the goal of getting them to start businesses. This is coupled with a year of mentorship that covers all aspects of running a company, from developing a business plan to marketing a product. "Prince Charles, through his Prince's Charities Canada, identified Based in Business as one of the best military entrepreneurship mentorship programs in the world," notes Almond, "and now he's getting behind them and helping them grow this project to additional locations across Canada."

While Enactus Canada works with young students, it also partners with industry and academia to fulfill its objectives. It is supported almost entirely by corporate Canada, generous individuals, and associations like the John Dobson Foundation. "Our organization sets itself apart because of its focus on experiential learning," says Nicole Almond. "Our students take their in-class experience and apply that knowledge to solve problems in their communities. Having achieved success in their own sectors, our academic and corporate partners appreciate the importance of this hands-on learning."

In addition to investing the first dollar, the John Dobson Foundation played a key role in Enactus Canada's development by working with it to pioneer the John Dobson Enactus Fellowship. This recognizes an elite group of faculty who, on their own time, without additional payment, act as coaches for Enactus Canada's student teams on campus. "Because of their efforts and dedication to the students' experience, the Fellowship recognizes those who meet certain criteria," says Almond.

"Because of the reputation that Dobson developed as a pioneer of entrepreneurial education, faculty are proud to say they are a John Dobson Enactus Fellow," she adds. Fellows are awarded a $1,000 stipend, but the vast majority direct the money to the community programs run by the students. To date, there are over 120 individuals who have been inducted to the John Dobson Enactus Fellowship.

"Before John Dobson agreed to start the Fellowship with us, we had virtually no involvement from faculty advisors or administrators of the institutions we dealt with," Almond notes. "His name, support, and stamp of approval all allowed us to be heard by the faculty and administrators, and we see this as a tremendous addition to the student experience. The John Dobson Fellowship has been critical to us in terms of growing sustainably."

Almond describes the academics with whom Enactus works as its "Entrepreneurial Faculty." "These people are really passionate about education. They're not just about the lecture, about telling students what to do. They want to show them and watch them grow as they experiment, try their own thing, build their own concepts and skill sets. They do things differently and look at education differently."

To celebrate the entrepreneurial spirit of young Canadians, Enactus Canada also runs an annual Student Entrepreneur National Competition, designed to highlight the success of full-time students operating businesses that are creating jobs and furthering investments in our economic future. Every year, student entrepreneurs present their businesses to panels of Canada's industry leaders in regional and national competitions in order to be named Enactus Canada's national student champion. That person then advances to represent Canada at the Global Student Entrepreneur Awards.

Enactus began running the program in the 1990s, and when it was at risk of being closed due to insufficient resources, the John Dobson Foundation helped to bail it out. "Thanks to the Foundation, students get access to a network of Canadian entrepreneurs and business leaders, media coverage, and recognition for their incredible achievements in business as they continue to pursue their post-secondary careers at the same time," explains Nicole Almond. "The Student Entrepreneur National Competition is the only program of its kind in Canada, and it is because of the John Dobson Foundation that the program is so successful."

"John Dobson and others understood how one young person, not just with a great idea, but with a great business, can totally revitalize an economy. We believe in them, and we celebrate their desire to pursue their business and academic dreams. If anything, there is greater potential for success because they are doing both."

There's a global element to the Enactus program, too. "Canada is one of thirty-eight countries that operate the Enactus program," says Almond. "Due to John Dobson's initial investment, which encouraged others to get involved, we were able to bring the international competition to Canada for the first time, in 2005. This is important because it put Canada, our organization, our students, and our entrepreneurs on the global stage. Today, we have solidified our place as a leader in our global network."

The Enactus concept is team-based, with each team including an executive member, project managers, faculty advisors, and John Dobson Fellows, who serve as coaches. More sophisticated teams have a business advisory board of local community leaders who mentor them.

Dobson was key to the organization's success. "We would not be where we are today without him," says Nicole Almond. "He believed in us and was there for us when we needed it. Not only did he invest his money, he helped engage others in our network and was a pillar of support for our organization and the values on which it rests."

∞ THE NEXT 36 ∞

The Next 36 is another startup organization that has received invaluable support from the John Dobson Foundation. It was launched with the goal of increasing Canadian prosperity by developing high-impact entrepreneurs.

Claudia Hepburn, co-founder and executive director of Next 36, says that the Foundation was quick off the mark when it was approached for seed money to start the venture. "We'd put feelers out to Ian Aitken about the John Dobson Foundation supporting us, and soon a cheque showed up in the mail. It was a great endorsement early on. This was in January 2010, months before our first board members' and founding patrons' donations arrived."

Hepburn said it was important psychologically to have the support of the John Dobson Foundation from the start, backed with more than just a promise. "We had lots of people saying good things and offering their support and promising they would give us financial support. To actually have a cheque arrive in the mail, with no strings attached, saying 'This is great, we believe in you,' was a vote of confidence early on." The Foundation's initial donation was $25,000.

The goal of the Next 36 is to develop the next generation of high-impact entrepreneurs in Canada. It selects thirty-six undergraduate students who are high achievers with a track record of entrepreneurship. It enrols them in a nine-month program, where they build ventures together in teams of four. Participants get access to CEO-level mentors, an investment of up to $80,000 in their business, access to support services, and academics from around the world to teach courses directly relevant to entrepreneurs. Hepburn explains, "We provide an extraordinary set of experiences and relationships for a small number of students who we believe have a high potential to build internationally competitive organizations." One venture founded by a Next 36 alumnus, Stephen Lake, has already earned renown as the most highly valued startup ever from famed Silicon Valley incubator, Y Combinator.

There are no other programs like Next 36 anywhere in the world, not with the level of resources or the focus on backing top under-grads as they are about to graduate from university, says Claudia Hepburn. "We give them a special level of investment resources, a special quality of academics, and the benefit of high calibre business leaders and entrepreneurs."

☞ THE MONTREAL ECONOMIC INSTITUTE (MEI) ☜

The John Dobson Foundation has also provided support to a number of think-tanks and groups of activists over the years, including the National Citizens Coalition (NCC), a conservative lobby group that campaigns in favour of smaller government and lower taxes while opposing the power of public-sector unions. It was headed by Stephen Harper from 1998 to 2002 before he re-entered electoral politics and became leader of the Canadian Alliance. Another long-time benefi-ciary of Dobson's support was the Vancouver-based Fraser Institute, a politically conservative think-tank with the stated mission of "to measure, study, and communicate the impact of competitive markets and government intervention on the welfare of individuals."

The Montreal Economic Institute, a think-tank founded in 1987 by a group of Quebec intellectuals and businessmen interested in pro-moting free-market ideas in the province, was also a beneficiary of Dobson's largesse. Initially a continuation of the Institut économique de Paris à Montréal, the new think-tank's activities really took off in the late 1990s with the appointment of Michel Kelly-Gagnon as exec-utive director. Playing a role similar to the Fraser Institute, the MEI established a leading place for itself in debates on Quebec economic policy and generates on average fourteen media mentions per day. With ten permanent staffers, it has produced research on a range of issues, including a groundbreaking ranking of Quebec high schools published in *L'actualité* magazine every fall from 2000 to 2008.

In 2004, the MEI was awarded the prestigious Templeton Freedom Award Grants for Institute Excellence based on its overall performance, including operating practices and public relations. The MEI is the first Canadian think-tank to be honoured by this award created by Sir John Templeton.

Michel Kelly-Gagnon, an entrepreneur himself who founded a company that did in-house training for large manufacturers before joining the MEI, first met Dobson in 1999 after being introduced by a mutual friend, investment manager Reford McDougall. McDougall felt Dobson might have an interest in supporting the Montreal Economic Institute, which until then had been struggling to gain traction.

"I remember our first encounter with John clearly," Kelly-Gagnon says. "McDougall had organized a lunch at the University Club down on Mansfield Street. At the time, I was using broad abstract language to describe the institution, referring to it as 'classical liberalism.' This university-type language did not agree with John, who interrupted me for clarification. But I repeated with my university language. He interrupted me again and directly asked, 'ARE YOU RIGHT WING?!' and I said, 'Yes,' and he said, 'Oh, okay, that's good.' He was always very straightforward."

Kelly-Gagnon soon came to appreciate Dobson's level of commitment to the fledgling think-tank during the Montreal Economic Institute's first big public event in December 1999. The keynote speaker was to be Stephen Goldsmith, mayor of Indianapolis, who had made his name as a reformer of urban America, credited with introducing new techniques to make public services more efficient. "The Institute had confirmed a whole bunch of journalists who weren't familiar with us, and we had confirmed the attendance of the mayor of Montreal, too," says Kelly-Gagnon. "This was to be our moment of truth! It was our launch. We had only two full-time employees at the time – me and an administrative assistant."

Goldsmith was due to fly in from Indianapolis, through Pittsburgh. Kelly-Gagnon received a call from his secretary at 10:30 a.m. with bad news: Goldsmith had missed his connecting flight and would not be able to make it. "Dobson's first contribution was

$10,000 as a sponsorship for this conference," recalls Kelly-Gagnon. "So I called him up and told him the speaker he had sponsored was stuck in Pittsburgh and that the event would no longer take place. He said, 'Well, get him down here!' I told him I couldn't. There was a silence, and then I heard him say some numbers. He ordered me to write them down. He said, 'That's my credit card. Use that to get a private jet to get him down here!' I thanked him and told him how much I appreciated it, and he said, 'Stop talking and get to work!'"

Kelly-Gagnon found a private jet and says the rest of the story was right out of a movie. "Goldsmith had to fly to St Hubert Airport, which is on the South Shore of Montreal. We were so late. The room was packed. I'm explaining the whole sequence to the guests, apologizing for the tardiness. As I'm speaking, an ovation begins, as Goldsmith walks in. So it went from a disaster to a dramatic success!"

Michel Kelly-Gagnon says the experience proved to be a big inspiration. "Now, whenever someone asks me something, I try to make decisions rapidly and try to act on these decisions rapidly. My approach to doing things without hesitation has been heightened by John Dobson and his model. For example, we'd discuss calling John Doe, and before I'd know it, he'd ask for the secretary to get him Doe's phone number immediately. I feel this philosophy explains his success. He was very action-oriented. Any two directors of the John Dobson Foundation can make a decision to have something happen, without the need to wait for a discussion and consensus. As a result, the Foundation has a quick turnaround approach, which has really made a difference for us and many other organizations."

Eschewing bureaucracy and lengthy application processes for funding, the John Dobson Foundation is lean and simple. "With John Dobson, we were able to have a conversation followed by a two-paragraph letter to get it approved," notes Kelly-Gagnon. "Sometimes it was a project, sometimes it was annual donations. It would vary. But the decision-making process was different from all other foundations that I knew."

According to Kelly-Gagnon, getting college and university students involved in entrepreneurial projects was Dobson's greatest contribution to Canada. "He often used the expression: 'MBAS are for managers of bean counters' and believed that, while many Canadians are interested in business administration, they are not so much interested in entrepreneurship. He always made a clear distinction between business schools, which he thought were inept, and actual entrepreneurial experience, which he valued. He believed many entrepreneurs would come more from arts, music, and so on, rather than business or engineering. In fact, most of the entrepreneurs of our era do not have formal educations in business administration."

Dobson's entrepreneurial spirit and hot-blooded approach made him different from most people Michel Kelly-Gagnon knew. "I've dealt with other successful people, but John was in his own category because of his no-bullshit and quick approach. We were like-minded people in terms of political philosophy, as well as spirit and mentality. I never knew either of my grandfathers, and John was the closest to a grandfather figure that I've ever had. That's the emotional-psychological relationship I felt toward him. It's more than just a business relationship."

CHAPTER 12

Looking to the Future

I am inherently very bullish, because I learned from
John Dobson that pessimists don't make any money.

— RANDY KELLY

As Formula Growth enters its sixth decade, Randy Kelly and John Liddy share a vision that sees the company continuing to thrive as an independent boutique investment firm. Harking back to Dobson's original concept, the idea is to stay small and focused on creating wealth for the customer through capital gains. "But the products have to change, because you have to give the customers what they want," says Kelly. "You have to evolve and try to keep your business model appropriate."

Kelly says that Formula Growth has been beating the market for fifty years and vows that it will continue to do so for another fifty years. "This is John Dobson's legacy. He beat the efficient-market hypothesis because he took advantage of everyone else being scared half the time and not being in stocks. This is especially true today when many people are afraid of stocks."

Kelly argues that people constantly misidentify or exaggerate risk. "They think they're going to get eaten by a shark or get hit by lightning. Like your worst nightmare, these things seldom occur. The only reason Formula Growth beats the market is because it tries to assess risk a little more correctly than other investors."

According to Kelly, history repeated itself in 2012 when trading volumes on the New York Stock Exchange were abysmally low. Stock market participation was also very low in 1984 when he joined Formula Growth because everyone remembered the steep drop of

1973–74 and the fact the Dow Jones was still at the same level it was in 1960. There was no money being made in equities. "It took from 1984 until 1996 for everybody to be 'all in' again," says Kelly. "I think we've got the replay going on again. Everyone's had it, and nobody wants to hear about stocks. I still feel it today, and you won't see anybody constructive about the stock market. I like that. Templeton always said 'blood in the streets.' I always thought that customers should buy us when we're down."

Randy Kelly says he's baffled as to why people don't want to own stocks. "Our investors are always worried about something. These days, everyone wants dividend stocks when Formula's stocks are growing their earnings fast, and earnings are the source of all dividends." Stock markets have historically generated returns of 8 per cent annually, above the average of economic growth of 3 per cent to 4 per cent. "If you're smart and don't mess around trying to totally avoid risk, you'll be Dobson and get almost 13 per cent and beat the market. That will aggregate to an enormous number over fifty years."

Formula Growth steers away from people who make "ridiculously conservative assumptions in order to avoid losses," Kelly notes. "I want to be in front of somebody who says he's got twenty restaurants, and can get to a hundred, then 300. Then I want to objectively assess his staff, his work ethic, his track record, taste his food, and, yes, see whether the bathrooms are clean! Then I want to watch him do it! I want to swing for the fences in a calculated and well-practised way."

Kelly notes that he's inherently bullish because he learned from Dobson that pessimists don't make any money. "I'm optimistic, because the CEOs I invest along with are inherently optimistic about their business, and they could give a damn about an earthquake in Japan, or Portugal's problems. They want to grow their business. I don't think the markets are risky over the long term. They're volatile in the short term because prices dance around so much on sentiment. Risk is low if you've done your work and you lengthen your time horizon."

In Formula Growth's view, occasional economic downturns are healthy because they purge the weak and give birth to new and vibrant businesses. "You've got to buy low. You have to be careful on your entry into a stock. But that's where it all happens," advises Kelly. "Get the entry price right, and then stick to your target price for your exit."

The basic tenets of good investing, championed by Formula Growth, remain unchanged. "Today, we have email, text messaging, but I'm doing the same thing," says Kelly. "It's better, quicker, but the philosophy is basically the same. Investing is the same. It's human emotions. It's assessing risk. It's diversifying your risks. It's about finding new, solid stories."

Formula Growth's original unit holders are now passing away, and while some units are being inherited by the next generation, their numbers keep shrinking as aging unit holders redeem their units. The Fund currently has about 450 unit holders, down from a peak of 1,000, while the average holding per client is about $400,000.

Since Randy Kelly became president in 1992, he has wrapped up the institutional fund, introduced hedge funds, and added marketing people. Formula Growth Ltd. is now controlled by Randy Kelly and John Liddy, who mainly runs the hedge funds from New York. The rest of the shares are spread around the staff. When staff members reach the age of sixty-five, their shares come back to the firm. As a result, the company is owned only by the people who work there. Kelly has shunned offers from outsiders to buy the company because he believes in the business model. "We punch way above our weight. As a firm with just over $500 million in assets, I think we do a good job, pound for pound. The younger guys are dialed into ownership to keep them interested and to make sure the entire team rows the boat forward together. There's a bonus on performance."

Taking ownership had always been Dobson's approach. "The staff members of Formula Growth are the biggest customers in Formula's products, that means everybody who works here," says

Kelly. "So when we're happy, the outside customers are happy, too." Kelly recalls that when he first met Dobson, he told him he would be getting into a business that could not be more challenging. "He told me to forget about the scientists, the Ph.D.s. The smartest people are attracted to Wall Street everywhere in the world. 'You're going to be in the toughest game you could possibly find,' he said. That's what really hooked me."

"John told me it was going to be a hell of a challenge, and that has turned out to be the case," muses Kelly. "There have been constant ups and downs and trying to beat the market. It's been a hell of a ride, culminating in a good record where we've created a lot of wealth for the customers."

⌘ A LIFE OF FUN ⌘

John Dobson never formally retired from Formula Growth, but by the second decade of the new millennium, he had not been active in its affairs for at least a decade. He remained chairman emeritus and was in constant contact with "the office." He also remained involved in running the John Dobson Foundation, helping to select worthy candidates for support while taking a keen interest in organizations and individuals already receiving support.

In 2010, he fell while walking in downtown Montreal, and during treatment, it was found that he had serious vascular blockages in his right leg that required amputation. In his last years, he was confined to a wheelchair in a well-appointed seniors' home a few miles from his beloved Square Mile, but he remained remarkably robust and passionate about current events and the ups and downs of the stock market. He was also in frequent touch with his large network of what he termed "my cronies," speaking frequently on the phone and receiving a regular stream of visitors, including old friends like Governor General David Johnston and Ian Soutar, and great boyhood mates like John Gray. In addition to listening to political commentators on television and the radio, he closely followed the PGA golf tournaments, having played on virtually every important course over the past seventy years.

Dobson also remained as opinionated as ever, vigorously criticizing things such as current US monetary policy, which he believed was crippling the greenback and dimming prospects for young people to have the same kind of investing success that he had enjoyed. But overall, he was happy in his own skin, grateful for the life he had led and the lucky breaks that came to him along the way. "I always believed in having fun, and I'm still having fun in my own way," he said with a gentle tone in his voice. "I've been fortunate to have always liked what I was doing, and to always have fun doing it. After all, to me, that is what life is all about."

On 24 July 2013, the day before his eighty-fifth birthday, Dobson fell ill and was admitted to the Montreal General Hospital for tests. Much to his frustration, he celebrated his birthday in the hospital. Five days later, he passed away peacefully in his sleep of congestive heart failure.

On 5 August, some three hundred people gathered in a chapel at Mount Royal Cemetery in Montreal to celebrate the life of their dear friend and colleague, in a service presided by the Reverend Robert Camara, rector of Saint George's Anglican Church in Châteauguay. Among those in attendance were boyhood pals, golf buddies, family members, Formula Growth unit holders, and the Formula Growth team.

Parker Knox, his nephew-in-law, spoke about the love Dobson had for family, business, politics, and Canada; about his visionary leadership; and about the personal influence Dobson had exerted on his own life. Diana Knox, his niece and closest survivor, described him as "one of a kind" and praised her uncle's giving nature and humility, noting that he did not want a big funeral or even a memorial service. Her daughters, Victoria and Alex, gave amusing anecdotes about their great uncle's quirks but also spoke of his constant curiosity and interest in young people. Ian Soutar and Randy Kelly both gave touching eulogies about how Dobson changed their lives and expressed gratitude for having known him for so many years.

At the front of the chapel were an urn containing Dobson's ashes – which were later scattered at his beloved Mount Bruno golf course, just like his sister Virginia's – along with his trusty golf clubs and bag, emblazoned with his name and decorated with flowers. The clubs were a reminder that, in addition to his remarkable achievements in business and his contributions to entrepreneurial education in Canada, golf was perhaps the greatest joy in John William Dobson's long and productive life.

Investing in the Course

Investing may have propelled John Dobson's professional life, and entrepreneurship education may have dominated his philanthropy, but when it came to his personal life, no passion was more central than the sport of golf. From the moment a visitor walked into Dobson's office at Formula Growth, the role of the game in his life was there for all to see: a set of golf clubs standing beside his desk, ready at a moment's notice to be hauled into action.

Since his teens, when John Dobson took up the sport at the Mount Bruno Country Club on the south shore of the St Lawrence River opposite Montreal, golf was seldom out of mind. "It's a disease," he readily admitted, describing golf as "a kooky game but a helluva good way to spend a life." A central part of Dobson's social life, golf also was the catalyst that got him to see the world, driving him to play at more than 600 separate golf courses around the planet, including premier courses in Australia, Japan, Latin America, as well as Scotland, the game's homeland.

For over half a century, golf proved its worth to Dobson as an unparalleled way to forge and maintain business relationships and friendships. "It's a networking game played all over the world," he said. "When you play golf with somebody for four hours, you get to know them a bit."

Wrapped up in this intense love of the sport was Dobson's profound attachment to the Mount Bruno Golf Club on the South Shore of Montreal. "I virtually grew up in Bruno," he noted, calling the club by its diminutive. When he was much younger, it would take no more than fifteen minutes to drive from the family home in Montreal's Square Mile to his beloved Bruno across the historic Victoria Bridge.

"He was a very highly regarded member of the Mount Bruno Country Club," says Drummond Birks, whose grandfather owned part of the property on which the course was built almost a century ago. (It opened in 1918.) "I think he was the second oldest member, but I had ten years on him. I was a third-rate golfer, and he was better and much keener." Indeed, as late as his mid-fifties, Dobson's handicap was in the low single digits.

According to Birks, the origins of the club date back to the late nineteenth century when Edson Pease, head of the Montreal office of the Merchants' Bank of Halifax (forerunner of the Royal Bank of Canada), decided to build a summer home on Mount Bruno because of its beautiful landscape and close proximity to Montreal. He asked two brothers from the Drummond family, who were running steel distributor Drummond McCall, to join him in making a bid for the property. One of the brothers was Birks's grandfather. In the early 1890s, the three friends built their homes on Mount Bruno, and Pease later became a prime mover behind the establishment of the Mount Bruno Country Club, even though he was not much of a golfer himself. In the contained world of Montreal's Anglo elite, Mount Bruno was seen as the Royal Bank's answer to the venerable Royal Montreal Golf Club, a bastion of the arch-rival Bank of Montreal. In fact, John's father, Sydney, who spent his career at the Royal Bank, was Mount Bruno's Country Club's president in the 1940s.

Brenda Norris, sister of John Turner, the former prime minister of Canada and long-time Dobson friend, recalls an amusing incident on the golf links dating back more than sixty years. "It was the summer of 1949 in St Andrews, New Brunswick, where we spent every summer, as did John and his sister Virginia. I was attempting to learn golf but wasn't much good at it and didn't much like it. Tennis was my sport. However, one of my current boyfriends was an avid golfer, and so I persuaded John to join us on the golf course. Every time my friend was either looking for his ball or looking the other way, John hit my ball for me. My beau was mightily impressed and years later, when I bumped into him (the romance didn't last!), he asked me if I was still a great golfer, and I replied, 'Of course!'"

In his hallmark red jacket, sweater, or polo shirt, John Dobson soon became a hugely popular player at Mount Bruno and elsewhere, known for his great sportsmanship and dedication to the sport. As a governor of the Royal Canadian Golf Association and an honorary director of the Quebec PGA, he was a big supporter of golf across the country. He also introduced a trophy for the winner of the annual Quebec Pro/Junior Golf Tournament, which for many years was held at Mount Bruno.

In 1975, Dobson helped to run the Canadian Open with John Churchill-Smith, a friend whose son Michael became Dobson's personal physician. It was being played at the Royal Montreal Golf Club where Dobson was not even a member, although Churchill-Smith was. It was very unusual for the chair of the Open not to be a member of the host club, but nobody was upset in this instance, such was Dobson's stature in the Quebec golf scene.

Dobson met many important and influential people on the golf course over the years and understood the value of developing strong relationships. He recalled once running into golf legend Jack Nicklaus ("The Golden Bear") during a tournament in Florida. "We weren't on the same team, but mine was running second to last. I went up to Jack and said, 'If you were on our team, we would be first!' He joked that he would have played with us if he wasn't already committed. How many people could have had such an encounter?"

On another occasion, during a game at Lake Nona in Florida, Dobson said he ran into Denis Thatcher, husband of then British prime minister Margaret Thatcher. The Canadian prime minister at the time was Brian Mulroney. "We had met several times before," Dobson recalled. "Anyway, he says to me, 'That boy you have up there is not very smart. He's managing everything wrong when it comes to South Africa."

Dobson also recalled playing golf with Robert Lowry, the Lord Chief Justice of Northern Ireland, at a course in Ulster. "We were on the ninth hole, and he had his bodyguards around. Suddenly, this golf ball comes bouncing around and hits Baron Lowry right in the face. I turn to a bodyguard and say, 'You're supposed to protect this man. What kind of a guard are you?' He thought it was pretty funny."

Golf was the centre of Dobson's social life, and it soon determined what he would do with his vacation time as well. For almost three decades, from 1968 to 1997, Dobson was a member of the Roger Bacon Golfing Society, a loose grouping of eighteen fanatics dedicated to playing "good" golf courses and meeting golfers "everywhere other than in Montreal." The society took its name not from the famous philosopher, but instead from a legendary nineteenth-century Scottish golfer of the same name.

During the Roger Bacon Golfing Society's history, members participated in thirty annual tours, during which they played 210 rounds of the game at 131 golf courses in Canada, the United States, England, Scotland, Wales, Ireland, Northern Ireland, and the Channel Islands. Golfers included members of the Royal Montreal Golf Club as well as Mount Bruno. Many were also members of the world's most prestigious clubs, thanks in large part to access facilitated by involvement in the Roger Bacon Golfing Society and the multiple connections of its members. Over the years, members played a total of forty-one matches against teams from twenty-five clubs and three societies, beginning at Royal Aberdeen in 1970, and the last one at Elie in 1996, both in Scotland. In the Bacon Chronicles, a privately distributed book recounting the history of the society, Dobson is satirically described as "a very noisy stock promoter renowned for sartorial elegance, in red."

John Gray, a friend since the 1930s, played golf with Dobson on countless occasions and praises his contributions to the Royal Canadian Golf Association. "We were keen to do better and occasionally had a good round. He was very interested in the game." Like other golf buddies, Gray became a unit holder of Formula Growth at its inception. "I believed in the integrity of the man. That's the only basis for investing in anything – to understand the people you're dealing with and to only deal with those you know have integrity. I'm not interested in some guy recommending something to me. I want to know that he has skin in the game."

Another long-time Dobson friend and Formula Growth investor, Edmond Eberts, ran the Turnberry Golf Tour from 1985 to 2004, an annual international invitational event. "The great Dobber – there was only one of him," Eberts enthuses. Eberts, who has authored several books on golf and is chairman and founder of Rapport Capital Formation Strategists Inc., went to Bishop's College School with Ian Soutar. Like Dobson, he also worked at C. J. Hodgson, opening their first Toronto office. He met Dobson around 1965, only a few years after Formula Growth was set up. In 1986, Dobson endorsed Eberts's nomination as a new member of the Royal and Ancient Golf Club of St Andrews, Scotland. "There are only 120 Canadians among the 1,800 members," Eberts notes.

Montreal art gallery owner Robert Landau met Dobson thirty years ago through golf at Mount Bruno and later joined him on golfing trips to Bermuda and Florida. Landau also became a Formula Growth investor. "A lot of people and members of the golfing fraternity invested in his Fund. I invested later within my capacity and over the long term, did very well. He had a very good track record, was always very honest and honourable," says Landau.

Still another of his golfing partners was Montreal dentist Frank Kay, who got to know Dobson through the sport and later invested with Formula Growth. (He also took on Dobson as a patient.) He recalls that early in their friendship, Dobson had invited him to play golf after someone in his Mount Bruno golf group had fallen ill. "He was a very persistent man. He called me at least five or six times! He convinced me to go to dinner and to go on a golf trip to Las Vegas. When I came back, I invested in Formula Growth. The first year there, I lost half my money. But he had a good track record, so I doubled up and did extremely well for the next thirty years. I was always impressed with his straightforward honesty. He and I basically had the same philosophy about golf as well – they tend to make golf courses too hard for no particular reason."

Dobson's tendency to be opinionated did not leave him on the links. "John's enthusiasm for this great game has never waned," Gregor Jamieson, director of golf at Florida's Lake Nona Golf & Country Club, wrote on the occasion of Dobson's eightieth birthday.

"He continues to make comments on the handicap system as well as the speed of greens. His opinion is that they are altogether too fast, which I concur with, as the skill level of most players is not good enough to be able to play at tour speed."

That passion for the game sometimes bordered on the foolhardy, according to former Formula Growth executive Peter Mackechnie. "We once played Castle Pines golf course just south of Denver, where they played the PGA International Tournament. There was this wild thunderstorm, and everyone was off the course. But Dobson was so determined to see it through. The bloody thunder and lightning were rocketing off the rocks by the side of the course, and by the end of the eighteen holes, we were totally drenched. I was really glad to be alive and relieved that I wasn't struck by lightning. Dobson walked in to the bar area, and like he always used to do, he would give his name first, 'John Dobson, Montreal.' And he said, 'I'm the special representative from the Royal Canadian Golf Association who rates the courses, and I would just like to tell you that this golf course that I played today ...' And I thought, 'John, how can you be saying this? It was raining so hard! We were running for our lives!' But he said, ' ... of all the golf courses that I've ever played around the world, this ranks in the top ten.' I felt so relieved because I didn't know what he might say, and I thought the members might hang him!"

Steve Farlow of Wilfrid Laurier University fondly remembers playing golf with Dobson a couple of times a year at Mount Bruno. "He absolutely loved playing golf, but the rule was that when you're out on the golf course, you don't talk business. He liked to play fast, have a nice dinner, and then talk business. To John, golf was golf. I can't tell you how much I enjoyed the five or six times I came to Montreal. We had a meeting at about 10:00 a.m. that would last maybe forty-five minutes. Then we'd be off in cars to Bruno for a quick lunch. Then out onto the golf course for the afternoon, followed by dinner. It didn't matter how well you played, but you had to know the rules of the game and play it properly. He didn't take his game too seriously, but as he aged, his scores would go up. He played very well. You wouldn't spend a lot of time looking for a golf ball. If it wasn't immediately apparent, he'd say, 'Let's move on, let's keep going.' He was focused on punctuality."

On the occasion of Dobson's sixty-fifth birthday in 1993, the Formula Growth team organized a surprise for him at Mount Bruno. As broker Robert Power recalls, "We had a great game and I was tasked with organizing it. There was a surprise party for him on the eighteenth hole. John and I came up and all his colleagues, friends, and members of the network were standing there holding up this big banner wishing him happy birthday. The eighteenth hole was a difficult one, and John just lined it up and sank it for par, straight and true like his character. I think he was very proud, and very touched."

Appendices

Formula Growth Fund Annual Performance

YEAR	FGF YTD	S&P 500 TR YTD	YEAR	FGF YTD	S&P 500 TR YTD
2012	12.6%	6.6%	1985	35.3%	31.7%
2011	(6.1%)	(8.7%)	1984	(11.8%)	6.3%
2010	23.8%	15.1%	1983	18.3%	22.6%
2009	41.5%	26.5%	1982	40.7%	21.5%
2008	(45.3%)	(37.0%)	1981	(5.1%)	(4.9%)
2007	0.6%	5.5%	1980	64.3%	32.5%
2006	10.2%	15.8%	1979	44.8%	18.6%
2005	7.5%	4.9%	1978	32.7%	6.6%
2004	9.0%	10.9%	1977	15.3%	(7.2%)
2003	59.3%	28.7%	1976	26.2%	23.9%
2002	(35.5%)	(22.1%)	1975	71.8%	37.2%
2001	0.7%	(11.9%)	1974	(36.2%)	(26.5%)
2000	(12.1%)	(9.1%)	1973	(34.5%)	(14.7%)
1999	26.5%	21.0%	1972	28.6%	19.0%
1998	9.5%	28.6%	1971	33.3%	14.3%
1997	20.9%	33.4%	1970	(24.6%)	3.9%
1996	25.2%	22.9%	1969	(7.5%)	(8.4%)
1995	37.3%	37.5%	1968	39.8%	11.0%
1994	(1.7%)	1.3%	1967	76.5%	23.9%
1993	27.8%	10.0%	1966	(15.9%)	(10.0%)
1992	27.5%	7.6%	1965	51.1%	12.5%
1991	72.8%	30.4%	1964	7.3%	16.4%
1990	(28.8%)	(3.1%)	1963	16.8%	22.8%
1989	24.9%	31.6%	1962	(28.7%)	(8.7%)
1988	13.2%	16.6%	1961	56.4%	26.9%
1987	(7.0%)	5.3%	1960	19.1%	3.9%
1986	13.5%	18.7%			

Formula Growth Fund Current and Former Employees

CURRENT EMPLOYEES (17) .... TITLE

René Catafago	Executive Vice-President, CFO
Nelson Cheung	Vice-President, Senior Portfolio Manager
Lucy Chher	Analyst, Trading, and Risk Management
Barbara Ellis	Manager, Administration, and Settlements
Cameron Fortin	Portfolio Manager
Michael Gentile	VP and Senior Portfolio Manager
Charles Haggar	VP and Senior Portfolio Manager
Randall Kelly	Chief Executive Officer, Co-Chief Investment Officer
Ari Kiriazidis	Vice-President Operations, Chief Compliance Officer
John Liddy	Executive Vice-President, Co-Chief Investment Officer
Rodney McCollam	Vice-President and Controller
Ahson Mirza	Research Associate
Marc-André Pouliot	Director, Risk Management and Client Servicing
James Sinclair	Portfolio Manager
James Soutar	Consultant
Anthony Staples	Vice-President and Senior Portfolio Manager
Rosanna Vitale	Administrative Assistant

FORMER EMPLOYEES (8)......................... TITLE

Mark Culver	Vice-President, Business Development
John Dobson..	Founder, Chairman
Debbie Gingras	Secretary
Kim Holden	Vice-President and Portfolio Manager
Peter Mackechnie..................................	Vice-President and Portfolio Manager
Darleen MacWhinnie	Secretary
Bette Lou Reade.....................................	Executive Vice-President and Portfolio Manager
Joanne Torch..	Secretary

FOUNDERS, DIRECTORS, ADVISORS (21) .... TITLE

Drummond Birks....................................	Director
Stuart Cobbett	Corporate Secretary, Director
Walter Cottingham	Founder, Officer, Portfolio Manager, and Consultant
Peter Cross	Founder
Roger DeSerres	Director
Nassie Godel	Director
Jacques Glorieux....................................	Founder, Director
Heward Grafftey....................................	Founder
John L. Grossman...................................	Consultant
Hugh Hallward.......................................	Director
Andy Hugessen	Founder
Neil Ivory..	Director
Donald Johnston	Corporate Secretary
Robert Midgley.......................................	Founder
John Rook	Founder
Frank Schnabel	Founder, Advisor
Lorne Webster...	Founder, Director
Ian Soutar..	Director and Consultant
Scott Taylor	Director and Consultant
Jacques Tétrault	Director
John Turner	Founder, Corporate Secretary

Index